INSIDE

LONDON

INSIDE

Discovering London's Period Interiors

Joseph, 1944–

JOE FRIEDMAN

Photographs by Peter Aprahamian

PRENTICE HALL PRESS

NEW YORK·LONDON·TORONTO·SYDNEY·TOKYO

LONDON

FOR JIM AND ISMAIL
AND WITH SPECIAL THANKS TO
CHRISTIANE

 Prentice Hall Press
Gulf + Western Building,
One Gulf + Western Plaza
New York, New York 10023

First published 1988
© 1988 Text Joe Friedman
© 1988 Photographs Phaidon Press Limited

Prentice Hall Press and colophon are registered
trademarks of Simon & Schuster Inc.

Library of Congress Cataloging in Publication Data

Friedman, Joseph
Inside London.

1. Interior decoration–England–London–History-
20th century. I. Title
NK2044.L6F7 1989 747.22′1 88-22579
ISBN 0-13-467465-0

Design by James Campus
Phototypeset by Tradespools Ltd, Frome, Somerset
Printed in Great Britain by
Ebenezer Baylis & Son Ltd, Worcester

10 9 8 7 6 5 4 3 2 1

page 1:
NO. 18 FOLGATE STREET, SPITALFIELDS
The peach-coloured late Georgian
bedroom (see page 58).

frontispiece:
ASHBURNHAM HOUSE, WESTMINSTER
Now a part of Westminster School, the Staircase
Compartment at Ashburnham House dates from before the
Great Fire of 1666, and is an early example of the classical
style revived in this country by Inigo Jones. It displays a
sophisticated use of space and ornament.

title page:
THEATRE ROYAL, DRURY LANE
Built to the designs of Benjamin Wyatt in 1811–12, the
monumental dome of the Theatre Royal, Drury Lane was
inspired by the Pantheon in Rome.

CONTENTS

INTRODUCTION

In the summer of 1986 I combed the London area for six hectic weeks in search of period locations for the Merchant-Ivory's screen adaptation of E. M. Forster's novel *Maurice*. The action is set in Edwardian times and all the locations needed to date from around the turn of the century. London is an ancient city with monuments stretching back to the Roman occupation. I thought my job would be an easy one, and I was right when it came to exteriors. The 'outside' of London is remarkably unspoilt in parts. There are streets, parks, and squares which are virtually unchanged since the eighteenth century. But the same does not hold true for interiors, and I soon discovered that it is rare for any interior, especially a domestic interior, to survive unchanged for more than ten or twenty years. Even where period interiors do survive, they are hard to find, since they are generally concealed from the street and invisible to the passer-by. My first instinct was to head for the library. For days I waded through history books and guides to London. Many of these dealt with London's architecture, and some described and even illustrated a selection of historic interiors, but to my surprise none dealt specifically with this subject. Friends and colleagues offered valuable advice, but in the end there was nothing for it but to knock on doors and invite myself in. It was a nerve-racking and often frustrating experience, including several near misses and many slammed doors. But the rewards were enormous. Behind the familiar and sometimes unprepossessing street fronts of buildings I had passed countless times before I encountered a thrilling range of unspoilt period interiors which had somehow escaped the ravages of modernization and redevelopment and which gave me a new insight into the history and character of London. By now I had caught some bug; today I cannot pass a building without peering through windows and opening doorways in the hope of finding some unknown architectural treasure. I decided to delve further. This book is the result.

Before I could begin I had to find a photographer. I wanted the book to be right up to date with original photographs showing interiors exactly as they survived. My first step therefore was to find someone who shared my enthusiasm for historic interiors; someone also who was prepared to rise at dawn and work late into the night if necessary to capture them when they were empty and unobstructed. Peter Aprahamian has been all these things. He could not have done a better job.

Greater London covers an area of some 600 square miles; there is an almost limitless range of types of interior; and although unspoilt examples are hard to find, there are many more than could possibly have been included in a book this size. This is not an exhaustive survey, but I have tried to be representative.

Most of the interiors are drawn from the centre of London, from the City, St James's, Mayfair, and Westminster, but many are located in outlying city areas, such as Brixton, Deptford and Finsbury Park as well as the suburbs and further reaches. In some cases I have come dangerously close to overstepping the boundary, and Londoners themselves may find it hard to believe that Carshalton and Charlton are really a part of the metropolis.

There is a great deal more to London's architectural heritage than a few city churches, the Houses of Parliament and Buckingham Palace. Some of the finest and most intriguing interiors in London are to be found in shops, hotels, restaurants, pubs, and cinemas – buildings often overlooked in conventional guides to London. It may seem odd that the book contains no photographs of church interiors, which are among the oldest and most important in London. However, I felt that there were far too many to choose from, enough to fill several volumes, and that the best were already well known. I wanted to get off the beaten track and break new ground, to feature interiors which had never before been published. I only wish I could have included more of the many sorts of interior which deserve greater attention, such as railway and underground stations, factory interiors, and even public lavatories (some of which have to be seen to be believed). Inevitably some of the interiors in this book will already be familiar, particularly to readers who visit historic buildings, but I hope that for the majority this will be a voyage of discovery, just as it was for me, and that even for those 'in the trade' there will be one or two surprises.

By period interiors I do not always mean interiors from the distant past. London has very few surviving interiors from before the Great Fire of 1666, and with one or two exceptions the examples I feature date from the late seventeenth century and after. Several were completed within living memory. The spectacular Art Deco barber shop at Austin Reed dates from the 1930s, the Italianate grotto at Malletts in Bond Street was built in the late 1960s, and Charles Jencks's Post-Modern mansion in Ladbroke Grove was completed as recently as 1981.

The process of selection was by no means fixed; it evolved along with the book. Looking back, however, I can see that there were certain considerations which remained with me from the start and which guided me throughout. The first was authenticity. I was looking on the whole for interiors which were more or less unspoilt, genuine well-preserved examples of specific periods and styles. It is an uncanny experience to walk off a noisy twentieth-century high street into a shop such as Martyn's, a grocer's in Muswell Hill, North London, where virtually nothing has changed in almost a century, not even the display of merchandize; stranger still to battle through the crowds in Kensington and, mounting the steps of Linley Sambourne House, enter a Victorian time-capsule undisturbed since the 1870s. I recognize that in the end there is no such thing as a totally authentic period interior, one which survives in its original state. Almost all have at some stage been altered or restored, and the tiny number which have remained untouched naturally show their age. I leave it to others to decide whether it is better to allow a brilliantly coloured interior to turn an antique shade of brown or to opt instead for restoration. This book contains examples of both approaches. I believe that to a greater or lesser extent all have retained their original character.

If I was drawn to the genuine, I was also attracted by the fake, or if that is too strong a word, the antiquarian: interiors of one period dressed up with fragments and furniture of another. The English have always excelled at this, and London is fortunate in having several outstanding examples, among them No. 18 Folgate Street, a house in East London, where every period from the early eighteenth to the late nineteenth century is magically evoked through an artful arrangement of antique furnishings. Equally beguiling is the Bride of Denmark, a model Victorian pub in the basement of the Architectural Press in Queen Anne's Gate, which was assembled around 1949 from fragments salvaged from gin palaces destroyed in the Blitz.

I know how frustrating it can be to gaze at photographs of beautiful places with no hope of visiting them, so I have tried to include as many interiors as possible which are accessible to the public. I do not imagine that people will flock to the Bond Street jewellers, Tessiers, as they do to the Tower of London. I cannot see busloads of tourists descending on Claridge's or Hoare's Bank; but I should like to think that since many of the interiors I feature are so central and can easily be visited in passing, some might be tempted off the beaten track. (For those unsure about exact addresses, transport facilities and conditions of admission there is a gazetteer at the back which provides all the relevant information.)

Many of the interiors in this book are by well-known designers and craftsmen, such as Sir Christopher Wren, Robert Adam, and Grinling Gibbons. However, the architectural history of London is not just made up of famous names, and some of my favourite interiors are by designers and craftsmen who are largely forgotten or whose names were never recorded. I cannot say who designed the Edwardian interior of F. Cooke's eel-and-pie shop at Dalston Junction in East London, still less identify the craftsmen responsible for its tiled and mirrored walls, marble-topped tables, and stained glass windows and skylights; but to my way of thinking the interior of Cooke's is just as valuable and worthy of preservation as any documented drawing room by Adam in St James's, perhaps more so, since it is quite unique, the only one of its kind.

One of London's great strengths is its ability to absorb foreign communities and cultures. This is likewise a strength of English architecture, which has always thrived on foreign influence. The interior of No. 6 Carlton House Terrace, the home of the Royal Society, is virtually indistinguishable from that of a Quattrocento Florentine Palazzo. The state apartments at Lancaster House consciously evoke the splendour of the Sun King's Palace at Versailles; and in the Arab Hall at Leighton House, with its Islamic tiles and lattice-work balconies and shutters, it is as if one had been transported to Cairo or Baghdad.

It is interesting, and sometimes astonishing, to see how interiors designed for one purpose have been converted to quite another; which explains why in almost every case I have grouped the interiors according to their present rather than their original function. Home House, for instance, a palatial Neo-classical mansion built for the Dowager Countess of Home by Robert Adam, is classified under Schools and Colleges, since it is occupied today by the Courtauld Institute, an art history faculty founded in the 1930s by textile millionaire and connoisseur, Samuel Courtauld. In the same way the Law Courts branch of Lloyds appears in the section on banks, although it started out in the 1880s as a restaurant and still preserves the exotic character of a late nineteenth-century banqueting hall.

Another characteristic feature of the English is their eccentricity and this too is reflected in their architecture. I can think of no better example than Lord Spencer's Room at Spencer House, an interior of the late 1750s which is currently being restored for use as an office. The chimney piece has been removed and the paintwork and gilding have been stripped from the plasterwork and panelling, but there is something undeniably dramatic about the bizarre screen of palm tree columns which were once flanked by marble blackamoors in pink togas brandishing bows and arrows. Equally outlandish is the Granada Bingo Hall in Tooting, once a cinema, which can only be described as a cross between a Gothic cathedral and a Moorish palace.

Behind a restrained conventional exterior the English sometimes conceal a Romantic nature. In the same way English architects have shown a tendency to secrecy and understatement in the design of facades, giving little hint of the gorgeous and sometimes outrageous interiors concealed within. The contrast in London beween street-fronts and interiors can be staggering. Who could guess that behind the establishment facade of the Royal Automobile Club in Pall Mall lies a torch-lit Byzantine-style swimming-pool? How many commuters are aware that high above their heads at Liverpool Street Station, in an obscure corner of the Great Eastern Hotel, bolted-doors draw back to reveal an Egyptian-style Masonic temple with lotus-leaf columns and a zodiac ceiling?

Condition was of small importance in relation to quality and atmosphere, and in a number of cases I foreswore rather ritzy interiors in favour of others which were shabby and even ruinous. Spencer House is one example. Cromwell House is another. The seventeenth-century staircase compartment, one of the oldest in London, is down to the brickwork in parts, and the treads of the stairs have become worn and bowed, but enough survives of the extraordinary carved balustrade to warrant a photograph, and the future looks bright since after long years of neglect the house is at last being restored.

Paradoxically, neglect is sometimes preferable to certain forms of restoration, and there are one or two historic interiors in London which I left out because I felt that they had been overdone. But there does come a point when neglect amounts to vandalism and photographing hardly seems worthwhile. I felt this point had been reached at Danson Park in Bexleyheath, a once magnificent eighteenth-century villa which the local council has allowed to fall into ruin. Mercifully the building has recently been acquired by a local architect, Laurie Taylor, who with the assistance of English Heritage has set about the daunting task of restoring it. He hopes eventually to open the house to the public.

Danson Park is one of many historic buildings which are currently being restored. There is a new awareness of the value of conservation and a growing interest in architecture and, more particularly, interiors. Even so there are no grounds for complacency. Danson Park illustrates the point that it is still possible for a major listed building to be run down and wrecked by a local authority. Interiors are especially vulnerable, since they are hidden from view and are therefore difficult to monitor. Sadly also they are not always accorded the same importance as facades. One of the interiors in this book, the Empire Theatre in Hackney, is under threat and in desperate need of funds. Another, the St Pancras Hotel, stands empty and neglected. A third which was photographed for this book was destroyed before publication and had to be excluded. Several more disappeared before I could record them, notably Rayne's in Bond Street, which once boasted a suite of Regency Revival showrooms by the outstanding post-war stage designer Oliver Messel. I myself saw Messel's distinctive display cases being hauled out on to the street (where are they now I wonder?) and a team of workmen stripping the interior behind a make-shift screen of brown paper hastily pasted to the windows. Thank heavens for the Dorchester Hotel, which with greater foresight and respect has held on to what must now be the only surviving Messel interiors in London, one of which, the roof-top dining room, is featured in this book. I only hope that this is not destroyed when the interior of the hotel is refurbished next year.

In writing this book my aim has been to turn London inside out so as to reveal some of its greatest and least expected treasures. I believe these to be a vital part of the city's architectural heritage, and if in any way I have contributed to their future conservation, this modest book will have done its job.

BINKS
STROLLED IN AS A KITTEN JUNE 1921,
AND PASSED OUT NOV. 14TH 1926
ADMIRED & LOVED BY EVERYONE

BATES,
HATTERS,
21, JERMYN ST

SHOPS

BATES, ST JAMES'S

*B*INKS, a stray from the streets of St James's, waltzed into Bates' hatters *(left)* one afternoon in 1921 and was instantly adopted. He has never left. Stuffed by the management after his death in 1926, he continues to preside over business from a position of honour on the shelf. The top hat and cigar are anything but fanciful – according to legend, Binks was never seen without them.

JAMES SMITH & SON, BLOOMSBURY

*E*VERY Londoner requires an umbrella, and there is no better place to buy one than James Smith & Son *(above)*. Founded in 1830, the shop moved to its present premises, a former dairy, in 1856 and little besides the stock has changed in the interim. Inside and out, Smith & Son is one of the sights of London.

HARRODS, KNIGHTSBRIDGE

*T*HE only serious rival to Allen's is the splendid Edwardian Meat Hall at Harrods *(left)*, a glittering tiled interior decorated with hunting scenes and peacocks. The interior dates from 1901–3, when the famous Brompton Road facade was erected, and has recently been restored, as part of a continuing programme of refurbishment.

R. ALLEN, MAYFAIR

*T*HE original owner had to fight a legal battle for the right to hang his wares in public. But it was worth it. At Allen's in Mount Street *(left)* merchandizing has been raised to the level of a fine art, the staff take as much trouble over the daily hang of meat as any artist composing a still life. The interior is more or less as it was when the shop first opened in 1887, with colourful glazed tiles and an oak counter surmounted by hunting trophies.

W. MARTYN'S MUSWELL HILL

*L*OCALS refer to Martyn's *(right)* as 'the Fortnum and Mason of Muswell Hill'. If only Fortnum's was as well preserved. The interior of Martyn's is virtually unchanged since the owner's great-grandfather started the business in 1897. Even the display of merchandize is in period. Particularly impressive are the display cases with finely wrought barley-twist colonettes.

AUSTIN REED,
REGENT STREET

*C*ONCEALED behind a sedate
Edwardian facade, the Art Deco
Barber Shop at Austin Reed is
one of the great secrets of
Regent Street. Oval in form,
with a continuous wave-scroll
ceiling light, it preserves its
original basins and chairs,
together with striking chevron
screens in chrome and frosted
glass. The floor is of Travertine
marble, the walls of pale blue
vitrolite. Altogether the most
complete interior of its kind in
London.

BERRY BROTHERS, ST JAMES'S

*B*ERRY Brothers *(above)* have been in business for over three hundred years and are still a family concern, best known for their excellent clarets and the Cutty Sark brand of whisky. The shop was built in the 1730s and stands on the site of a late seventeenth-century coffee shop, whose original painted sign still hangs outside. The floor dips alarmingly in parts and the walls are lined with antique letters.

Since 1765 the scales on the right have been used to weigh celebrities, and nine leather-bound volumes contain the facts on such distinguished former customers as the poet Byron and Napoleon III.

TESSIERS, BOND STREET

*T*ESSIERS *(right)* opened on Bond Street in 1852 but the business was founded much earlier in the eighteenth century by Lewis Tessier, the grandson of a Hugenot exile said to be descended from the Kings of Sicily. In Victorian times Tessiers were not only jewellers and silversmiths, but 'artists in hair', and examples of their work still hang above the mahogany and looking-glass display cabinets on the right. No one should be deceived by the gas mantels projecting from the mirrors. These were introduced in 1973, when an industrial dispute led to crippling power cuts which left the rest of Bond Street in darkness. Ironically this is almost the only thing at Tessiers which has changed.

MALLETTS, BOND STREET

*T*HE last thing one expects to find in a smart antique shop is a grotto, but in the minds of the management at Malletts grottoes and antiques seem strangely connected. Both their branches of business have showrooms of this kind. The first *(above)*, in Bond Street was designed by architect Raymond Erith in 1968, and is said to have been inspired by a similar interior at the Villa d'Este in Rome. The second *(right)*, at Bourden House in Davies Street, is made up almost entirely of shells and was completed as recently as 1975.

RESTAURANTS

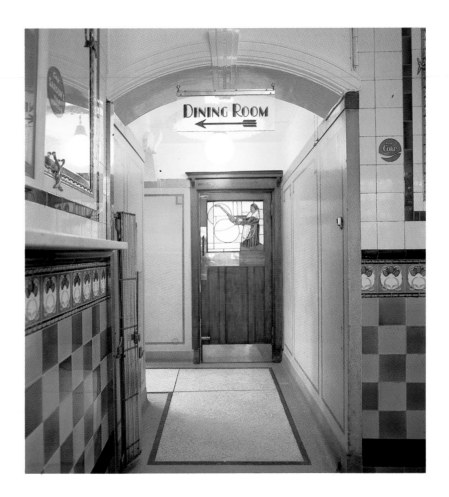

F. COOKE, DALSTON

*T*HIS traditional eel-and-pie shop *(above and left)* is one of the great sights of London. The interior dates from around 1910 and features stained glass windows and skylights, Baroque Revival plasterwork, marble-topped tables, and tiled and mirrored walls. Hats off to the Cookes, who have maintained the place through four generations.

CAFE ROYAL, REGENT STREET

*A*N atmosphere of sensuality and scandal still pervades the crimson and gilt interior of the Grill Room at the Café Royal *(overleaf)*, once the haunt of playwright Oscar Wilde and his circle. The interior dates from the 1860s and is among the earliest of its kind in London, featuring a Rococo Revival ceiling with inset painted panels and mirrored walls divided by caryatids supporting vases.

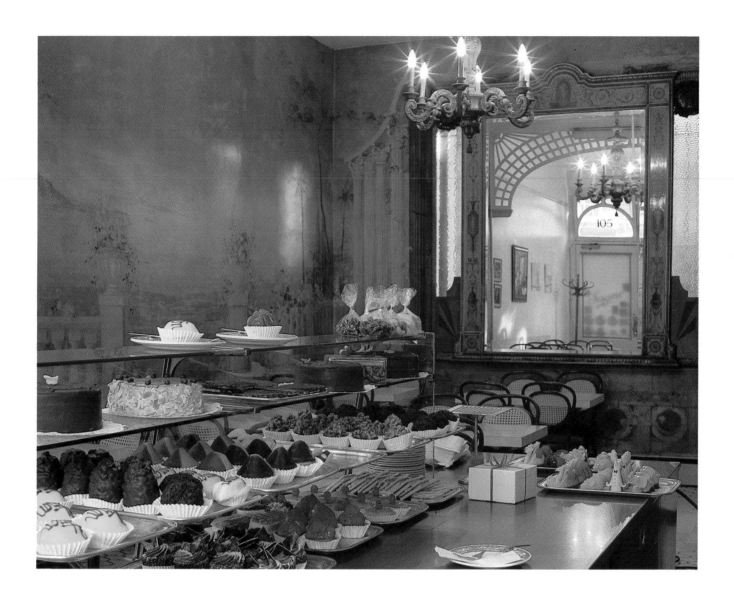

RULE'S, COVENT GARDEN

*S*AID to have been the favourite restaurant of Edward VII and his mistress Lily Langtry, Rule's is little changed since it opened in the 1890s, and the principal dining room *(left)* has immense period charm and atmosphere. Back stairs lead to private dining rooms on the upper storeys.

SAGNE'S PATISSERIE, MARYLEBONE

*S*AGNE'S was founded in the early 1920s by an immigrant Swiss pastry-lover, and despite several changes of ownership it retains a strong continental atmosphere. The walls are painted with classical landscapes and ruins, and a fine Pompeian-style mirror hangs opposite the door.

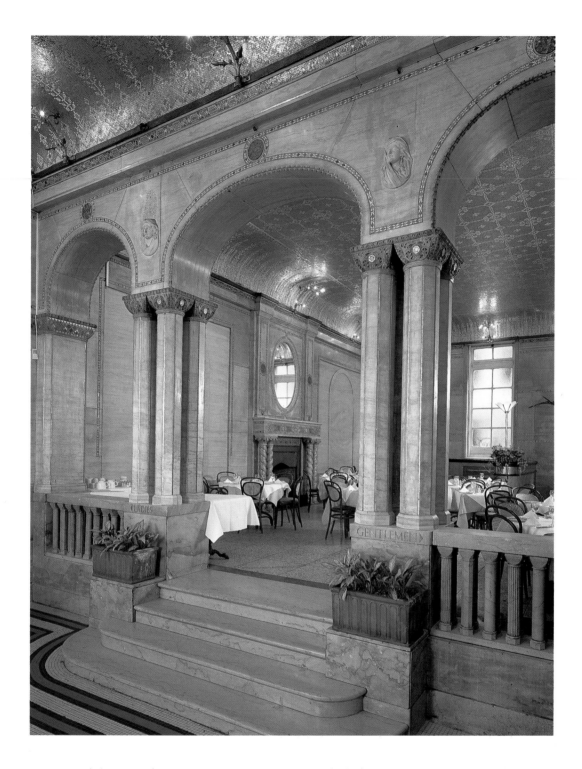

SIMPSONS IN THE STRAND

*S*IMPSONS started out as a chess club in the 1820s, but by the time the present building was erected in the 1890s it had become the 'Simpson's Grand Divan Tavern'. The ground-floor Dining Room is a baronial affair in the Arts and Crafts style, with inlaid panelling, but the first-floor is occupied by a suite of Neo-classical interiors in the style of Robert Adam. The best of these *(left)* has delicate lunettes set into a barrel-vaulted ceiling, pastel-green panelling, and original benches and tables.

THE CRITERION BRASSERIE, PICCADILLY CIRCUS

*S*TEPPING into the Criterion Brasserie is like stepping into a painting by Klimt, but for years this resplendent interior lay concealed behind hardboard panels and a suspended ceiling. Now that it has been exposed and restored we can all admire the Moorish arcades and gilt mosaics, which date from Edwardian times.

RISTORANTE ITALIANO, MAYFAIR

*T*HIS unpretentious Italian restaurant occupies the ground and first floors of a terraced house in Curzon Street. The ground floor has been modernized but on the first floor is a Rococo interior *(above)* which must once have been an extremely fancy drawing room. The walls are divided into carvilinear, scrollwork panels, ornamented with scrolls, foliage and musical trophies, reminiscent of the style in vogue in France during the reign of Louis XV. The interior probably dates around the time of the *Entente Cordiale* (1904), when the warmth of Anglo-French relations brought about a revival of this style.

HOTELS

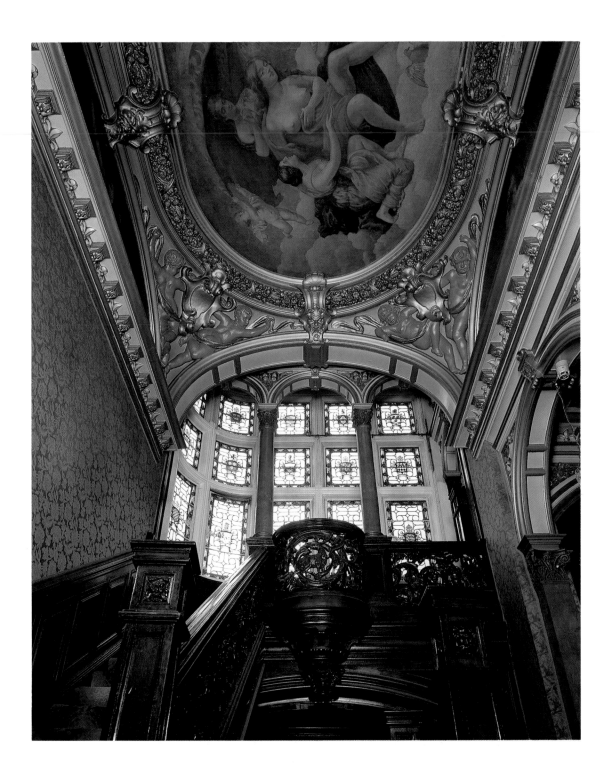

INVERNESS COURT HOTEL, BAYSWATER

*N*OW a hotel, this Bayswater mansion was reputedly built as a love-nest for a Victorian businessman and his mistress. They obviously enjoyed a rich and varied relationship. The interiors range in style from early Georgian to Louis XVI and there is even a bar-room composed of boxes from a disused continental music hall.

Quite what the architect had in mind in the Staircase Hall *(above)* I cannot say. The gilded putti and the allegorical ceiling painting are recognizably baroque, but the stained glass windows and the richly carved balustrade might have come from some late medieval manor house. Well worth a visit.

THE SAVOY HOTEL, THE STRAND

*M*UCH of the Savoy Hotel has been remodelled and modernized. The principal rooms have been redecorated, but there are corners of the building where time appears to have stood still. The busy lobby *(left)* linking the front and rear areas of the hotel, is almost exactly as it was when its designer Basil Ionides completed work in 1929.

The recess contains a stylish fitted bench, the terminals forming volutes, and is faced with looking-glass etched to represent a fountain. The chandelier is original, too.

CLARIDGE'S, MAYFAIR

*I*N the public rooms at Claridges anyone who abides by house rules can enjoy the very best in Art Deco design. Meticulously maintained by the management and staff, this is the best preserved of London historic hotels. The side entrance *(above)* is characteristic of the glamour and excellence of the decoration, supervised by Basil Ionides in the mid-1920s.

DORCHESTER HOTEL, PARK LANE

*T*HE Dining Room above is one of a suite of interiors at the Dorchester by the outstanding post-war stage designer Oliver Messel and was completed in 1953, Coronation Year. The room is conceived as a temple to Bacchus, the god of wine, who presides from a baldaquin over the chimney piece. Gilded foliage covers the mirrored walls, and in the far right-hand corner, nearest the door, a caged bird suggests that in Messel's imagination diners at the Dorchester were so many birds in gilded cages. The hotel will shortly be closing for drastic refurbishment. It would be a tragedy if Messel's suite was in any way disturbed.

PARK LANE HOTEL, PICCADILLY

*I*T is the easiest thing in the world to pop one's head through the ballroom entrance of the Park Lane Hotel on Piccadilly and take in the remarkable Jazz Age Foyer *(right)*, completed to the designs of Henry Tanner in 1927. The interior is virtually complete, with original murals and stylish silver-framed chairs and sofas.

THE GREAT EASTERN HOTEL, LIVERPOOL STREET STATION

A Pharaonic burial chamber? A set for *The Magic Flute*? The Freemasons' Temple *(above)* at the Great Eastern Hotel could be mistaken for both. Built in 1912, this solemn and little-known interior is still in use. When meetings are in session all the lights are extinguished except for the central star. The effect is positively eerie.

ST PANCRAS HOTEL, EUSTON

*T*HE staircase at the St Pancras Hotel *(right)* combines two great nineteenth-century passions: engineering and Gothic architecture. Completed to the designs of Sir George Gilbert Scott in 1878, it is a monumental construction in iron and stone with ochre walls stencilled in gold with fleurs de lys. For years the building has stood empty and neglected. The landlord, British Rail, promises restoration. But when?

CLUBS AND SOCIETIES

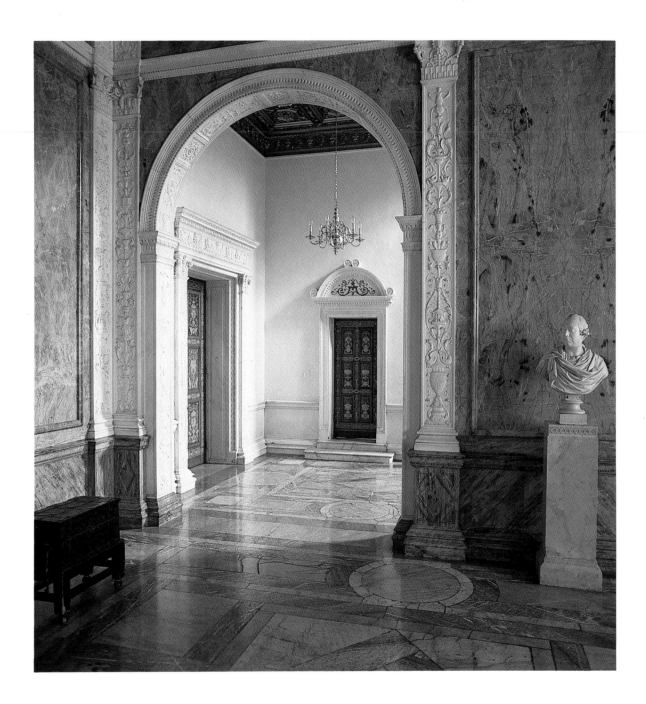

THE REFORM CLUB, PALL MALL

COMPLETED in 1841, the top-lit colonnaded Hall of the Reform Club *(left)* is a breathtaking example of the Italian Palazzo style, with polychromatic decoration in a dozen different colours and materials. The club was founded in 1836 by champions of electoral reform, but in the course of time politics has politely been removed from the agenda.

ROYAL SOCIETY, CARLTON HOUSE TERRACE

THE Entrance Hall of the Royal Society *(above)* is virtually indistinguishable from that of a Quattrocento Florentine palazzo. The exquisite marble carvings and inlaid doors might have been commissioned by Lorenzo di Medici himself. In fact they were made around 1890 for Argentine millionaire C.H. Sandford, whose extravagance extended to the erection of a mother-of-pearl ceiling over the main staircase.

THE ATHENAEUM CLUB, PALL MALL

A statue of Apollo presides over the stately Grecian entrance hall
of the Athenaeum Club, completed in 1830 to the designs of
Decimus Burton, best known for the Ionic Screen at Hyde Park
Corner. No less august is the Library *(above)* piled from floor to
ceiling with rare editions in exquisite bindings.

ROYAL AUTOMOBILE CLUB, PALL MALL

*B*UILT in 1909–11 by the Anglo-French partnership of Arthur
Davis and Charles Mewès, the Royal Automobile Club *(overleaf)* is
a curious but typically Edwardian amalgam of different styles. The
facade is Louis XV, with a backward glance at Gabriel's
colonnaded buildings in the Place de la Concorde in Paris. The
dining room is Louis XVI, with a wealth of late eighteenth-century
French detail. But most spectacular of all is the torch-lit
swimming-pool in the basement which can only be described as
Byzantine. Descending the staircase one instantly feels like an extra
in an epic motion picture by Cecil B. de Mille, or a classical sybarite
in a suggestive painting by Alma Tadema.

TRAVELLERS' CLUB, PALL MALL

*F*OUNDED in the years after Waterloo as a meeting
place for travelled English gentlemen and their
distinguished foreign guests, the Travellers' Club has
always been associated with a cultivated, cosmopolitan
view of the world. The building was designed by Sir
Charles Barry, architect of the adjoining Reform Club,
(qv). The facade heralded the arrival of the Italian
Palazzo style, but the interior was more diverse, the
Library *(left)* combines a replica of an ancient Greek
frieze with Roman columnar screens grained in imitation
of light oak.

BROOKS'S CLUB, ST JAMES'S

*S*CRUPULOUSLY restored after a recent fire, the great
Subscription Room at Brooks's is one of the most elegant
interiors in clubland. It is also one of the earliest, dating
from the late 1770s and was designed by the architect
Henry Holland. The simplicity and restraint of the
interior, its simple geometry, and the shallow relief of the
plaster decoration are typical of Neo-classical design in
the generation after Robert Adam.

PUBLIC HOUSES

THE SALISBURY, HARINGAY

*T*HE decoration literally spills out on to the street from this late Victorian gin palace in north London *(left)*. Fruity tile-work porches lead through to a cavernous bar room, best seen through a dense cloud of cigarette smoke at closing time.

YE OLDE CHESHIRE CHEESE, FLEET STREET

*W*ITH its blackened walls, open fire, and bare floor boards strewn with sawdust 'Ye Olde Cheshire Cheese' *(above)* is everyone's idea of a traditional London tavern. A sign over the front door announces that the building was erected in the late seventeenth century and legend has it that Samuel Johnson was a customer, compiling his 'Dictionary' over ale and biscuits.

THE RED LION, ST JAMES'S

*T*HE interior of The Red Lion (*above*) has all the ingredients of the classic Victorian pub: etched glass, carved and polished woodwork, and a Lincrusta (embossed paper) ceiling. Sadly interiors of this sort are fast disappearing. Most of London's pubs are owned by breweries and other corporations which tend to impose a uniform house style on all their properties, often replacing genuine period fittings with vulgar reproductions.

THE BLACK FRIAR, BLACKFRIARS

*B*UILT by the architect H. Fuller Clarke in 1905, the Black Friar is a uniquely fine example of an Arts and Crafts pub. The interior is in an excellent state of preservation with grinning figures and bronze reliefs on a mock monastic theme by distinguished sculptor Henry Poole.

THE BRIDE OF DENMARK, QUEEN ANNE'S GATE

Not so much a pub; more a private bar. The Bride of Denmark occupies a warren of basement rooms in the eighteenth-century headquarters of the Architectural Press in Queen Anne's Gate and is only open to members of staff and their guests. No one should be fooled by the decoration. The interior *(above)* was assembled around 1949 from fragments of Victorian pubs destroyed in the Blitz. The lion looks none the worse for wear.

DOMESTIC INTERIORS

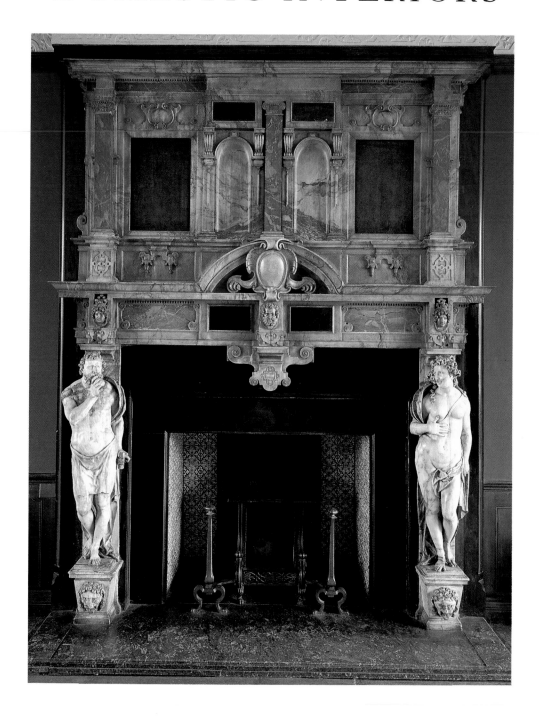

CHARLTON HOUSE, GREENWICH

*C*HARLTON is a typical Jacobean manor house, erected in 1607–12 for Adam Newton, tutor to Prince Henry, the son of James I. The building has served a multitude of purposes – today it is used as a local community centre – and yet much of the original decoration survives intact, including the magnificent chimney piece above, carved in marble with figures of Vulcan and Venus and attributed to the sculptor Nicholas Stone.

No. 18 Folgate Street, Spitalfields

*A*T No. 18 Folgate Street, an early eighteenth-century house in Spitalfields, East London, American Dennis Severs has succeeded resurrecting the past, magically evoking the eighteenth and nineteenth centuries through a series of antiquarian interiors decorated in every style from the reign of Queen Anne to that of Queen Victoria. Especially beguiling are the late Georgian bedroom *(see page 1)* in a glorious peach colour; the abandoned Victorian garret *(right)* hung with cobwebs and crimson velvet; and the mid-eighteenth century Dining Room *(above)* which resurrects exactly the confusion of a drunken dinner party depicted in a painting (attributed optimistically to Hogarth) over the chimney piece.

HAM HOUSE, SURREY

*E*VERYTHING survives at Ham: the architecture, the gardens, the furniture, even the archives. This has enabled the National Trust, which owns the property, and the Victoria and Albert Museum, which acts as administrator, to recreate the original appearance and atmosphere of this remarkable seventeenth-century relic. The house was built for Sir Thomas Vavasour, whipping boy to Charles I, but most of the interiors date from the 1760s when Ham was occupied by the Duke and Duchess of Lauderdale, whose bedchamber is pictured above.

SOUTHSIDE HOUSE, WIMBLEDON COMMON

*C*ONTROVERSY surrounds the interior of Southside House *(right)*, which some believe to be genuine but which may well be antiquarian, an artful combination of antique furnishings and fragments assembled in the nineteenth century. Personal favourites are the candle-lit 'Elizabethan' Dining Room and the 'Renaissance' Hall. But there are many more and since the house is sometimes open to the public, it is best to explore – and decide – for oneself.

OSTERLEY PARK HOUSE, ISLEWORTH

*O*STERLEY is a sixteenth-century manor house remodelled in the second half of the eighteenth century by Robert Adam. The so-called Etruscan Room *(above)* is a typically eclectic fusion of ornaments derived from a variety of classical sources, including Greek vases and Pompeian wall paintings.

ORLEANS HOUSE, TWICKENHAM

*T*HIS octagonal garden pavilion is all that remains of Orleans House *(right)*, an eighteenth-century Thameside villa occupied between 1815–17 by Louis Philippe, Duc d'Orleans later King of France. The Octagon was designed by the distinguished English architect, James Gibbs, best known for the church of St Martin-in-the-Fields, Trafalgar Square. The decoration is in the Baroque style with virtuoso plasterwork by Italian stuccatori.

MARBLE HILL HOUSE, TWICKENHAM

*T*HIS elegant Palladian villa, reproduced here by kind permission of English Heritage, dates from the 1720s and was built for the Countess of Suffolk, a mistress of George II. Small in scale, but exquisitely proportioned and finished, Marble Hill has all the characteristics of a doll's house. A finely carved staircase leads up to the Great Room *(above)* a perfect cube with paintings of Roman ruins by Panini, gilded plasterwork and woodwork, and a typically formal arrangement of early Georgian furniture.

SOANE MUSEUM, LINCOLNS INN FIELDS

*W*HEN architect Sir John Soane bequeathed his house to the nation in 1837 he did so on condition that nothing be disturbed, that the interior remain exactly as he left it. His wish has largely been fulfilled and the visitors can still experience at first hand the romantic, not to say eccentric, atmosphere of this early nineteenth-century museum house. The first-floor Drawing Room *(right)* has recently been restored to its original brilliance, with lemon-yellow paintwork and upholstery. The Breakfast Room *(overleaf)* on the ground floor is more subdued. The shallow dome with incised geometric ornaments and the use of indirect lighting are typical of Soane's work, as is the use of indirect lighting, mirrors, and the tantalizing perspectives.

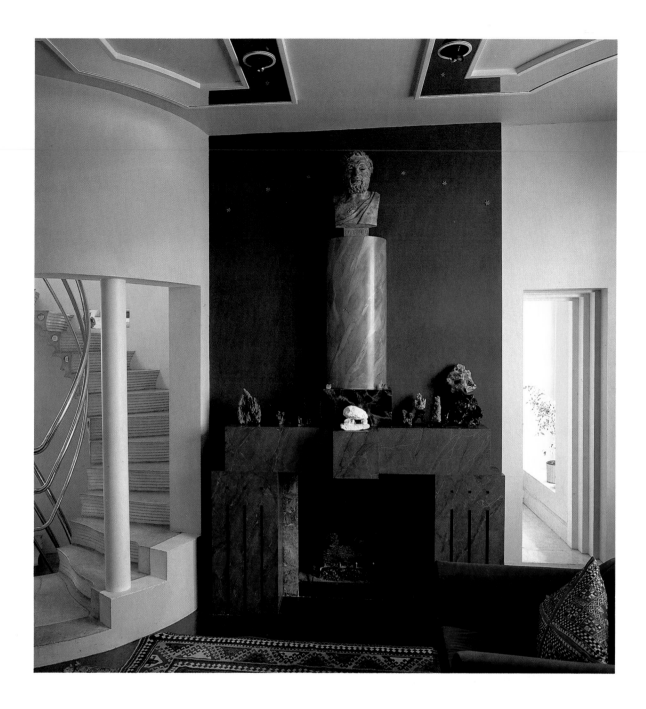

THE THEMATIC HOUSE, LADBROKE GROVE

Designed by the partnership of architect Terry Farrell and architectural thinker and *eminence*, Charles Jencks, this Post-modern mansion in Ladbroke Grove is a unique example of what its owner (Jencks) describes as 'radical eclecticism'. Pressure of space forbides me from entering into an exposition of the elaborate symbolism at work in the interior above.

LINLEY SAMBOURNE HOUSE, KENSINGTON

Linley Sambourne House *(overleaf)* is far and away the most atmospheric historic house in London, a Victorian time-capsule undisturbed since the 1870s. With its Bohemian jumble of furniture and objects, its ageing paintwork and upholstery, this unique example of the 'Artistic' style of decoration has an authenticity possessed by few other historic houses anywhere in the world.

LITTLE HOLLAND HOUSE, CARSHALTON

Without the timely intervention of the local council this Arts and Crafts house would have fallen prey to a local developer and the Sitting Room *(above)* would have been converted into a garage. Instead it has been restored and opened as a public museum. Begun in 1902, Little Holland House was designed and built by self-taught artist-craftsman Frank Dickinson, a disciple of Ruskin and Morris, who lived here until his death in 1963. Everything was hand-made by Dickinson.

LEIGHTON HOUSE, KENSINGTON

In the Arab Hall at Leighton House, originally the home of Victorian painter Sir Frederick Leighton, it is as if one had somehow been transported to Cairo or Baghdad. The Islamic tiles are antique, some dating from the seventeenth century. When the sun streams through the lattice-work shutters and water trickles from the fountain in the centre I long to loll on the damask-covered benches and summon my hookah-pipe and belly-dancers.

Studio House, Chelsea

*I*N the nineteenth century, long before
it was colonized by Sloane Rangers
and Punk Rockers, Chelsea was a community
of artists and writers, and its streets are
still lined with studio houses, one of
which has remained in the same
Bohemian family for almost a century
and is more or less unchanged. Electric
light has been introduced, bringing a
modicum of modern comfort to the
interior (note the frolicking putti
supporting light bulbs), but sputtering
gas fires threaten to reduce the place to
ashes.

THEATRES AND CINEMAS

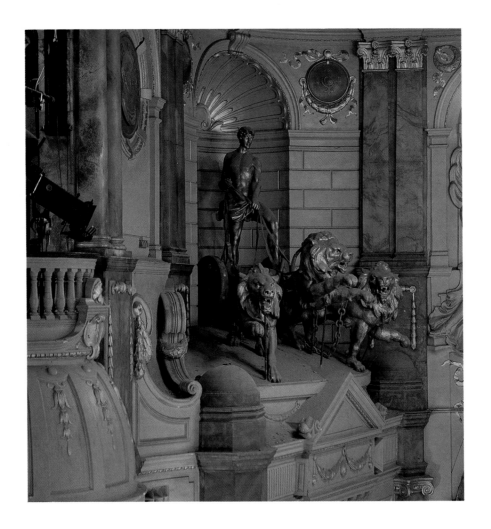

THE COLISEUM, ST MARTIN'S LANE

*B*UILT in 1903–4 for theatrical impresario Oswald Stoll the Coliseum was originally a music hall but it has been occupied since 1968 by the English National Opera Company. The vast auditorium seats over 3,000 spectators, but with most eyes fixed on the stage or the audience, superb architectural details such as the lion-drawn chariot and charioteer *(above)* can sometimes be overlooked.

THE EMPIRE THEATRE, HACKNEY

*W*HEN film director Franco Zeffirelli launched his screen adaption of Verdi's *La Traviata*, he announced that he was taking 'Opera to Texas'. Frank Matcham, the architect of the Empire Theatre, did likewise, bringing the opulent decoration of Italy's great opera houses to a music hall in Hackney *(right)*. The Empire opened in 1901, but was later acquired by the Mecca organization and converted into a Bingo Hall. It has recently been acquired by a local preservation trust, which is doing all it can to raise the £150,000 required to complete the purchase and restore the theatre to its original use and splendour.

THE PLAYHOUSE THEATRE, EMBANKMENT

*A*FTER careful restoration, the interior of the Playhouse is much as it was when the theatre first opened in 1906. Its construction involved a large contingent of French designers and craftsmen, whose presence can still be felt in the light-hearted Gallic decoration of the walls and drop curtain. An ingenious detail is the sacrificial ox skull in the Doric frieze by the exit, which despite its ancient classical origins has been wired as an electric wall light.

Academy Theatre, Brixton

Nothing, not even the spectacular Art Deco Foyer above, prepares the visitor for the outrageous decoration of the auditorium of the Academy Theatre, Brixton. Below a ceiling painted to represent a star-lit sky, the proscenium arch and wings form an elaborate Mediterranean villa-and-garden complex, complete with statues, balconies, loggias and artificial trees and vegetation.

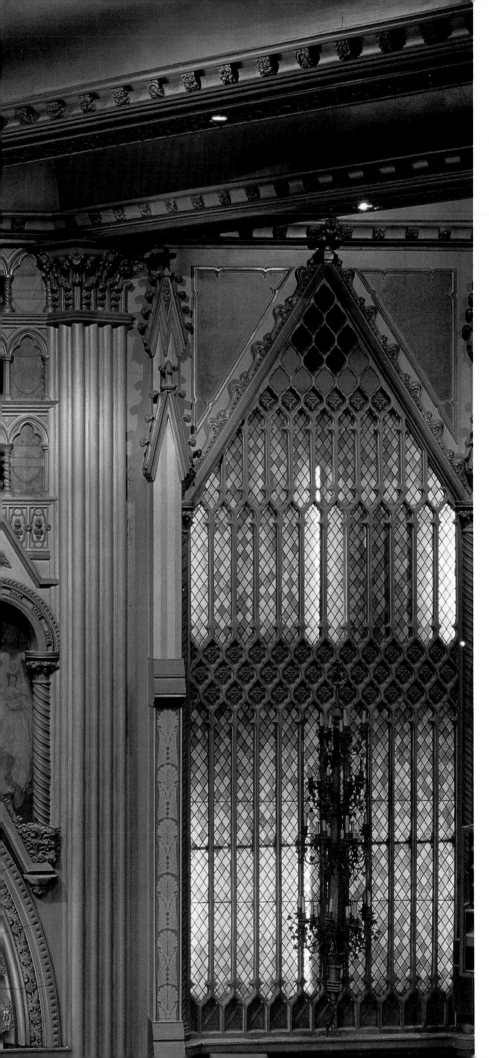

GRANADA BINGO HALL, TOOTING

*T*ODAY we would call it escapist, but in the
1920s and 30s the word was 'atmospheric'. Of all
the 'atmospheric' cinemas built in London at
that time, the Tooting Granada, which operates
today as a bingo club, was the most splendid.
The architect, Theodore Komisarjevsky, saw it
as his mission to supply cinema audiences with
'the flavour for romance for which they crave'.
At Tooting he certainly succeeded. The
auditorium is conceived as a medieval
Cathedral, with stained glass windows, Gothic
tracery and frescoes; the foyer evokes the
atmosphere of a baronial hall; and the Hall of
Mirrors is like something out of the Alhambra
Palace.

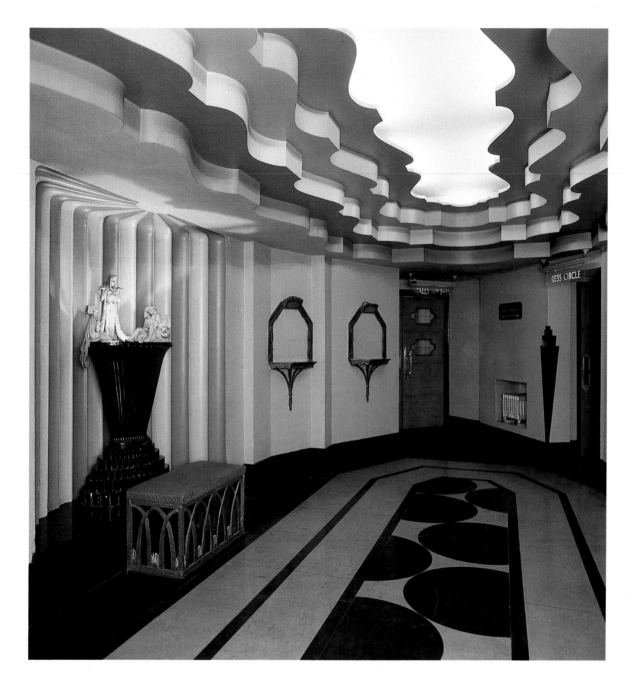

New Rainbow Theatre, Finsbury Park

MOST of London's great cinemas have either been subdivided or converted into bingo halls. The New Rainbow Theatre (originally the Astoria) is unusual in that it serves as the headquarters of a branch of the Pentecostal Church. The decoration of the Foyer *(right)* is straight out of the *Arabian Nights*, but the atmosphere is more like 'the morning after'. The fountain in the centre is defunct, and flooding has caused serious damage to the paintwork in the dome. There are plans to spend between six and ten million pounds restoring the building. The sooner the better.

Savoy Theatre, The Strand

DESIGNED by Basil Ionides in 1929, the Savoy is the finest and best preserved Art Deco theatre in London. The auditorium retains its original carpet and cut velvet seat covers, but the most exciting interior is probably the rear entrance *(above)*, which combines a unique 'whirlpool' ceiling and a geometric inlaid marble floor with an Egyptian-style trophy and a metalwork bench ornamented with shells.

OFFICES

LICHFIELD HOUSE, ST JAMES'S

BUILT in the 1760s by James 'Athenian' Stuart, Lichfield House was the first terraced house in London to boast a Greek temple facade, with engaged columns copied from the Erectheion on the Acropolis. The interior was similar in style, but it was overlaid in the 1790s by another architect, Samuel Wyatt, and there are parts of the building where it is hard to distinguish between the two phases of decoration. The top-lit Staircase Hall (*above*) is a case in point. Since 1856 the building has been occupied – and well maintained – by the Clerical, Medical and General Life Assurance Society.

SPENCER HOUSE, ST JAMES'S

SPENCER House – a Portland stone palace overlooking Green Park – was built in the mid-eighteenth century for John, 1st Earl Spencer. It has functioned as an office building since the 1950s and is currently being restored. The interiors range from the Palladian to the Neo-classical, but no stylistic label fits Lord Spencer's Room, which with its bizarre screen of palm-tree columns is one of London's greatest architectural curios. An analysis of the paintwork has revealed that the walls were originally green, with the frieze picked out in white and gold. The coffering in the alcove was a mixture of all these colours plus pink. The frieze is copied from the Temple of Antoninus and Faustina in Rome, an appropriate choice since its principal ornament, the griffin, is also the Spencer family device.

No. 8 Clifford Street, Mayfair

*I*LLUSIONISTIC murals decorate the walls of this early Georgian town house, which has served in its time as a tea shop and operates today as an office block. The panel on the left has been attributed to Sir James Thornhill, Serjeant Painter to George I. The awkward fit would suggest that it had been cut down and might even have been intended for a different setting.

Cromwell House, Highgate

*A*FTER long years of neglect Cromwell House is at last being restored for use as an office building. The Staircase *(right)* is thought to date from around 1640 and may well be the earliest in London. The principal feature is the balustrade, carved with military and heraldic ornaments celebrating the achievements of the original residents.

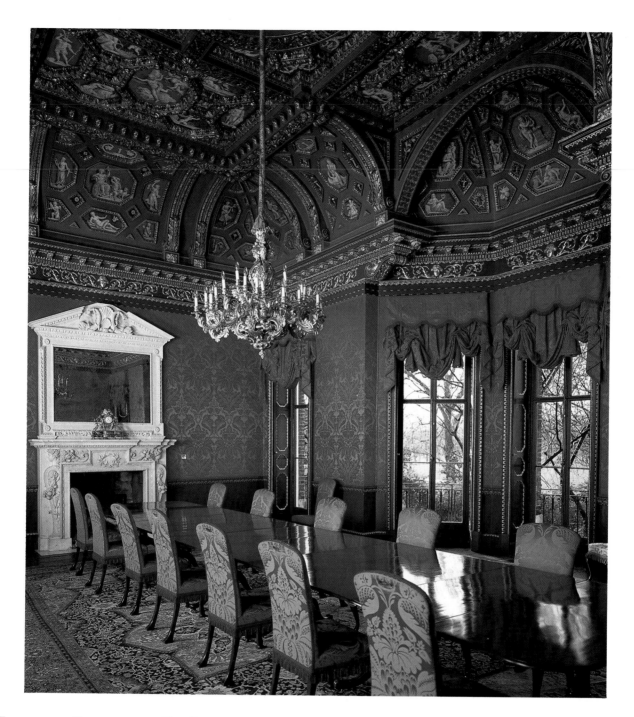

LLOYDS REGISTER OF SHIPPING, THE CITY

*T*HE interior of Lloyds *(left)* is a curious blend of the Edwardian Baroque and the Arts and Crafts, with painted ceilings apparently inspired by Michelangelo's Sistine Chapel at the Vatican. The architect was Thomas Colcutt, the versatile designer of Simpson's-in-the-Strand (see Restaurants), and Frank Brangwyn was among the artists responsible for the decorative paintwork. Note the colossal marble and tile-work chimney piece and the futuristic chandeliers.

WILLIAM KENT HOUSE, ST JAMES'S

*D*ESIGNED by the architect William Kent, this mid-eighteenth century mansion was originally the home of Prime Minister Henry Pelham. Today it functions as the London headquarters of the Eagle Star insurance group, which has lavished millions on its restoration. Crimson damask lines the walls of the opulent Palladian Board Room *(above)*, which retains its original marble chimney piece and overmantel and its coved and coffered ceiling painted with classical figures.

OAK ROOM, (THAMES WATER AUTHORITY) ISLINGTON

*T*WICE dismantled and rebuilt, this late seventeenth-century Board Room is situated today in a 1920s office building in Islington occupied by the Thames Water Authority. Originally it formed part of Cistern House, the headquarters of a company set up in 1613 to bring fresh water to London from unpolluted sources in Hertfordshire.

The carvings over the chimney piece, a detail of which is seen on the right, are by Grinling Gibbons, who collaborated with Sir Christopher Wren on the decoration of St Paul's Cathedral. The ceiling is ornamented with exuberant Baroque plasterwork and a painting representing the Apotheosis of William III. The curious object on the top right-hand shelf is a section of wooden tubing which was used to channel water before the introduction of metal piping.

DAILY MAIL, FLEET STREET

CARMELITE House, a Victorian Gothic office building off Fleet Street, has been occupied by the *Daily Mail* since its construction in 1899, but the newspaper will shortly be moving premises. The management have already decided to dismantle and rebuild the Board Room, a unique example of Napoleonic style of decoration with pedimented mahogany bookcases. But there seems no possible way of transporting the Staircase Hall *(above)* which features an ornate ironwork balustrade and lift shaft and rare Art Nouveau murals representing allegorical figures and great men of literature. I only hope the *Daily Mail's* successors show proper restraint.

DAILY EXPRESS, FLEET STREET

IN designing the entrance hall of the Daily Express building in Fleet Street the architect Robert Atkinson somehow managed to combine the form of a medieval chapter house with the metalwork finish of a spaceship. Particularly striking are the allegorical reliefs representing colonial enterprise and the chromium-plated handrail on the staircase taking the form of serpents. As with Carmelite House (see Daily Mail) a question mark hangs over the building's future since the *Express*, like the *Mail*, will shortly be moving premises.

BANKS

HOARE'S BANK, FLEET STREET

*T*HE Banking Hall at Hoare's *(above)* is virtually unchanged since its completion in the 1830s. Original customers would instantly recognize the magnificent oil burning stove, rising from the centre of the stone-flagged floor, capped by a classical lamp and decorated with a Greek Revival frieze of gilded honey-suckle. Protective screens have not been allowed to disfigure the beautifully finished counters, and the porters still wear period costume.

BANK OF ENGLAND, THE CITY

*T*HE Court Room (right) built in the 1700s, is all that survives of the old Bank of England, which was demolished and greatly enlarged in the 1920s and 30s by the architect Henry Baker. The room was designed by Sir Robert Taylor, and is typical of his style, combining Classical and Rococo elements. But Taylor would probably have had difficulty finding the interior, let alone identifying it, since it has been removed from its original position on the ground floor to its present location on the first and has otherwise been altered and 'improved'.

BARCLAYS BANK, PICCADILLY

ONE would never guess that the spectacular oriental-style interior of No. 160 Piccadilly *(above and right)* had been designed as a car showroom; it is hard enough to believe that it functions today as a bank. Free-standing red lacquer columns support a vaulted ceiling, while the floor is inlaid with concentric black and white stars in marble. The counters and furniture are of black and red lacquer with Chinese ornaments in gold. The oriental theme is continued in the manager's office *(right)* which could be mistaken for the counting house of some eighteenth-century trader in Canton.

LLOYDS BANK, THE STRAND

BUILT in 1883, the Law Courts Branch of Lloyds Bank was originally a restaurant and club for lawyers. Lloyds took possession in 1895, but the Entrance Hall *(overleaf)* is much as it was originally, with exotic virtuoso tilework by Doulton's. The building stands on the site of a seventeenth-century tavern called 'The Palsgrave Head' in tribute to Frederick Palsgrave, King of Bohemia, who married Elizabeth Stuart, daughter of James I. Portraits of the King and Queen appear in the decoration of the foyer, together with characters from the plays of dramatist Ben Jonson, who was a regular customer.

HOSPITALS

ROYAL HOSPITAL OF CHELSEA

FOUNDED in 1682 as a home for army veterans and disabled heroes, the Royal Hospital of Chelsea is London's answer to the Hôtel des Invalides in Paris. The Hall and Chapel, by Sir Christopher Wren, are familiar sights, but few visitors are allowed to see dormitories. The carpet and curtains are modern concessions to comfort and privacy, but otherwise the Long Ward *(above)* remains more or less unchanged.

GROVELANDS PRIORY HOSPITAL, SOUTHGATE

*P*ICTURED on the left is the remarkable vaulted Breakfast Room at Grosvenor Priory, an elegant Neo-classical villa built by John Nash in 1798, which has recently been converted into a private clinic. The room is painted to represent the interior of a bird cage set in an idyllic landscape. *Trompe-l'oeil* interiors of this date and style are extremely rare.

THE OLD OPERATING THEATRE, ST THOMAS'S HOSPITAL, SOUTHWARK

*T*HE operating theatre at St Thomas's Hospital (*overleaf*) dates from 1821, long before the introduction of anaesthetic, and is the oldest surviving interior of its kind in England. Remarkably the room is located in the attic of the Chapter House of Southwark Cathedral and once served as an apothecary's herb garret. It was bricked up in the mid-nineteenth century and only rediscovered in 1956. On display is a gruesome array of antique surgical instruments and a box of sawdust designed to catch the blood that dripped down from the operating table. Notice also the blood-stained apron in the corner and the sign on the far wall which reads '*Miseratione Non Mercede*' (Act out of compassion, and not for gain).

SCHOOLS AND COLLEGES

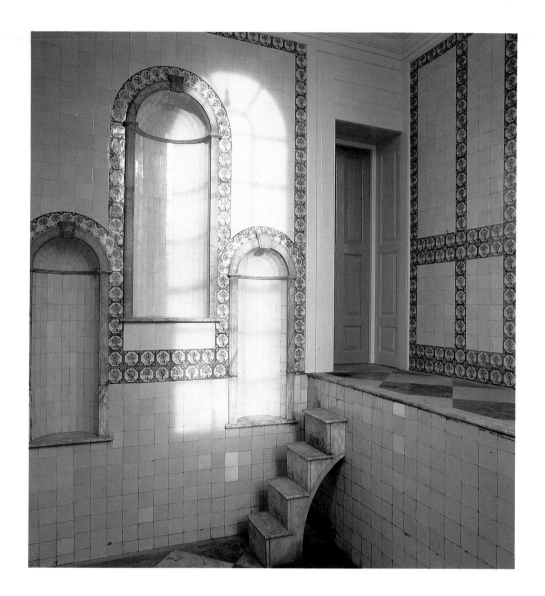

St Philomena's Convent, Carshalton

*T*HE Bathroom at Carshalton House *(above)* must be one of the earliest interiors of its kind in London. Completed in 1720, it is situated in a free-standing water tower in the grounds and it is decorated with original Delft tiles imported from Holland. Five marble steps lead down to a huge Roman-style bath measuring eight feet by eleven.

HARROW SCHOOL

*C*OMPLETED around 1615, the Fourth Form Room at Harrow
(above) provides a grim reminder of the rigours of education in the
early seventeenth century. Originally the school took only forty
boys, all of whom gathered here for lessons under the watchful eye
of the Headmaster and his assistant. Over the centuries departing
Harrovians have been encouraged to carve their names on the
panelling and furniture, with the result that there is graffiti here by
such distinguished former pupils as the poet Byron, and several
Prime Ministers, including Peel and Churchill.

COURTAULD INSTITUTE,
PORTMAN SQUARE

*R*OBERT Adam built this palatial Neo-classical mansion in 1773–6,
but since 1931 the building has been occupied by the Courtauld
Institute, an art history faculty founded by textile millionaire and
connoisseur, Samuel Courtauld. The climax to Adam's design is
the Staircase *(above)*: a towering top-lit construction decorated
with illusionistic murals and grisaille panels by Angelica
Kauffmann and Antonio Zucchi.

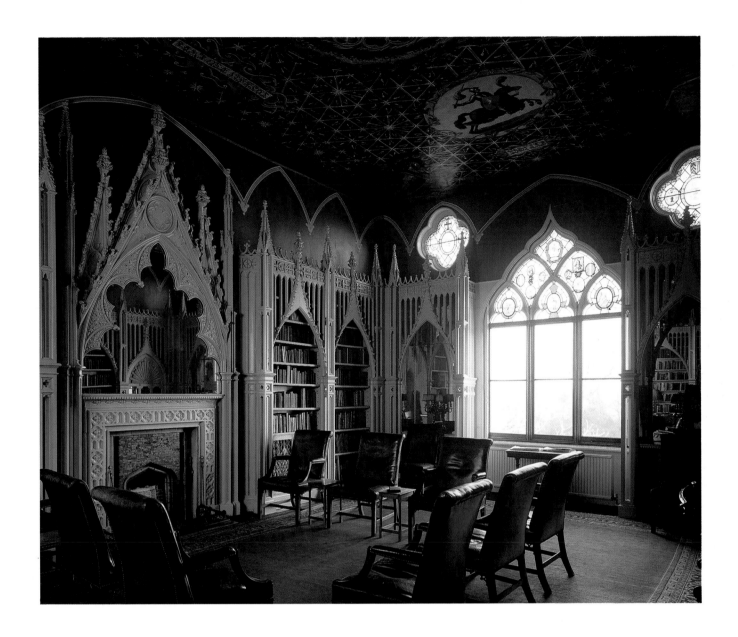

STRAWBERRY HILL, TWICKENHAM

*S*TRAWBERRY Hill is a castellated Gothic Revival villa built in the second half of the eighteenth century for wit and connoisseur Horace Walpole. The building is used today as a school, but the interior is well preserved with a wealth of Gothic detail culled from a bewildering variety of medieval sources. Revivalism in the arts, the resurrection of past styles, is something one associates with the Victorian age. Strawberry Hill shows that this fascinating phenomenon began much earlier.

THE RICHMOND FELLOWSHIP, HOLLAND PARK

*B*Y the turn of the twentieth century the construction of grand houses in London had passed out of the hands of the aristocracy and into those of wealthy middle-class businessmen. This town house of 1905–06 with its peacock-coloured decoration, was originally the home of department store millionaire Sir Ernest Debenham. Debenham's architect was Halsey Ricardo, but the Domed Hall *(right)* was largely the work of Gaetano Meo, and George Jack, who added the Byzantine-style mosaic ceiling and balconies in 1913. The tiles are original and produced by William de Morgan. Some are reputed to have come from the Tzar of Russia's yacht, *Livadia*.

GOVERNMENT AND CIVIC BUILDINGS

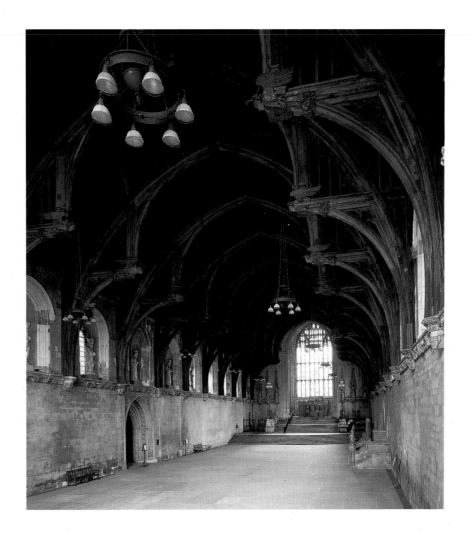

DEPTFORD TOWN HALL

*A*FTER an absence of almost two hundred years the Baroque style returns to London and flowers as never before in the giddy-making Staircase Hall of Deptford Town Hall *(left)*, built to the designs of architect Charles E. Rickards in 1902–05. The mermaids flanking the entrance to the Council Chamber are a reminder of Deptford's ties with the port of London. Only the lantern seems out of place, an inverted umbrella which might have come from Brighton Pavilion.

WESTMINSTER HALL

*W*ESTMINSTER Hall is one of London's oldest surviving interiors. The foundations and lower portions of the walls are Norman and date from the end of the eleventh century. The masonry and carpentry *(above)* are the work of Henry Yvele and Hugh Herland and were added in the reign of Richard II around the turn of the fourteenth century. The Hall has been the scene of some of the most momentous events and ceremonies in English history, including the trials of Guy Fawkes and Charles I. Weighing 600 tons, the lofty hammerbeam-roof is supported by massive external buttresses and is the earliest example of its kind in England. Stone figures of English Kings line the south wall under the protective gaze of carved wooden angels bearing shields.

LANCASTER HOUSE, ST JAMES'S

*B*EGUN in 1825 for Frederick, Duke of York, younger brother of George IV, Lancaster House was completed in 1838 by the Duke of Sutherland, whose descendants sold it in 1912 to soap millionaire Sir William Lever. Lever did the patriotic thing and presented the house to the nation as a suitably impressive setting for state functions. Many of the interiors date from the 1820s and are decorated in the 'Louis Quatorze' or 'Versailles' style. The Staircase Hall *(above)* is later, an interior of the 1830s, equally opulent, but Italian in inspiration rather than French.

HOUSE OF LORDS, WESTMINSTER

*T*HE construction of the House of Lords began in 1840 and involved some of the greatest artists and craftsmen of the day. The walls of the Princes' Chamber *(right)* are decorated with bronze reliefs by William Theed representing important events from Tudor history and with portraits by Frederick Crace of Henry VIII and his wives.

FOREIGN OFFICE, WHITEHALL

*T*HE Durbar Court *(overleaf)* completed in 1866, originally formed part of the India Office, and was open to the sky, with bear pits let into the floor to give it a suitably sub-continental atmosphere. A glass roof has since been added and the floor covered over in marble. The interior has recently been restored.

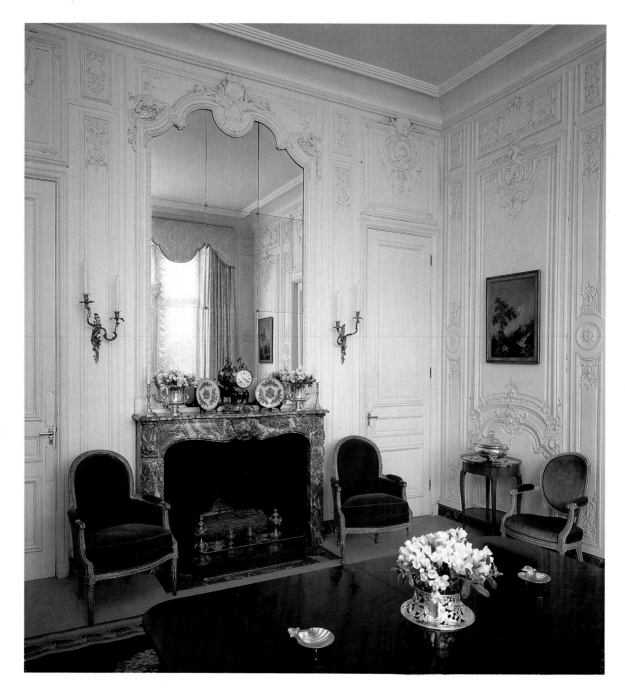

THE FRENCH AMBASSADOR'S RESIDENCE, KENSINGTON

*B*UILT in 1840 for the Duke of Marlborough, No. 11 Kensington Palace Gardens was acquired by the French in 1944. The interiors are decorated throughout with seventeenth- and eighteenth-century French furniture and pictures, and the walls of the Private Dining Room *(above)* are clad with Louis XV panelling rushed to London from a château near Paris in preparation for a presidential visit shortly after the Second World War. France may be a republic, but the decoration of its London embassy is unashamedly *Ancien Régime*.

THE BRAZILIAN AMBASSADOR'S RESIDENCE, MAYFAIR

*S*INCE 1940 Plymouth House in Mount Street has been the official residence of the Brazilian Ambassador to Britain. The house dates from the late 1890s and takes its name from the man who built it, Lord Plymouth, a wealthy industrialist and collector. Much of the marble used in the decoration of the dramatic Entrance Hall and first-floor Lobby *(above)* came from Plymouth's own quarries at Penarth. It is quite the most spectacular embassy in London.

LIVERY HALLS

APOTHECARIES' HALL, BLACKFRIARS

*T*HE Apothecaries' Company was founded in 1617 and is still involved in the education and examination of pharmacists. The Hall *(above)* was built a few years after the Great Fire, on the site of an earlier building, and much of the woodwork is original. A minstrels' gallery at the north end is surmounted by the royal coat of arms, while a portrait of Gideon Delaune, apothecary to Queen Anne, hangs in a prominent position below, accompanied by a chest donated by one of the company's founding members, William Clarke.

STATIONERS' & NEWSPAPERMAKERS' COMPANY, AVE MARIA LANE

*F*ROM 1557 to 1710 all books legally published in England had to be registered with the Stationers' Guild, which also had the honour of burning heretical books. In 1933 the Stationers merged with the Newspapermakers, and today the team devotes its energies to charitable work. The Hall *(right)* dates from 1673 and retains its original carved screen. Armorial and military flags hang from projecting shafts in the wall, and figures associated with literature and printing, appear in the stained glass windows, which were added in 1888.

DRAPERS' COMPANY, THROGMORTON STREET

*T*HE Drapers' Hall *(left)* may not be the oldest livery hall in London – it was built in 1902–10 – but it is certainly the grandest, and the Company has every reason to be proud of its recent restoration. The ceiling is painted with scenes from Shakespeare (the central panel depicts a scene from *The Tempest*), but the overall effect is that of a Roman arena.

ARMOURERS' AND BRAZIERS' HALL, MOORGATE

*P*IKES, shields, and coats of armour are proudly displayed on the walls of the Armourers' and Braziers' Hall, laid out here for an official banquet.

The building dates from 1840, but the history of the company can be traced back to the early fourteenth century. The Armourers and Braziers at one time controlled the trade in brass and copper articles, as well as edged tools, guns and armour. Their connection with metal is maintained today through the funding of research in metallurgy.

THE FISHMONGERS'
COMPANY,
LONDON BRIDGE

*T*HE Fishmongers' Company has
been in existence for over seven
hundred years with a hall near
London Bridge since 1434. The
present hall was completed in 1834
and is a fine example of Greek
Revival architecture and
decoration. Despite extensive bomb
damage during the Second World
War and subsequent restoration,
the Drawing Room is particularly
impressive. Much of the furniture is
original, including a giltwood
console table supported by
dolphins, which serves as a
reminder of the Company's
connections with fishing and the
sea. One would never guess that
this and other interiors at the
Fishmongers' Hall had virtually
been rebuilt after catastrophic
bomb damage in the Blitz.

ACKNOWLEDGMENTS

My thanks must go first of all to James Ivory and Ismail Merchant who, in letting me loose on London in search of period locations for *Maurice*, first gave me the idea for this book. To my partner Peter Aprahamian, I owe an enormous debt of gratitude for months of excellent work, sometimes under conditions more conducive to mental breakdown than to good photography. No one could have brought more enthusiasm to the project, or greater tact, than my assistant Christiane Sherwen, whose support and encouragement were invaluable.

I have had the benefit of expert advice from a number of specialists in the field of architectural history and interior decoration. For giving so generously of their unique experience and knowledge, I should like to thank: Colin Amery, Clive Aslet, Marcus Binney, Dorothy Bosomworth, Stephen Calloway, Dan Cruickshank, Colin Cunningham, Dudley Dodd, Antony Feldman, Michael Gillingham, Mark Girouard, Roderick Gradidge, Stephen Jones, Michael Pick, John Martin Robinson, David Mlinaric, Joseph Morduant Crook, Alan Powers, Anne Saunders, Alistair Service, Gavin Stamp, Peter Thornton, Clive Wainwright, David Watkin and Roger White.

My thanks must also go to all the many local historians and borough councillors to whom I wrote for suggestions and who supplied me with much useful information: Barry Arden, Peter Barber, D. J. Catford, Mr Ellis, R. J. Evans, Gwynydd Gosling, J. Harding, P. Harness, Carl Harrison, R. J. Huntley, A. V. Mascull, David McDonald, Lilian Noble, A. J. Robinson, D. A. Ruddom, Joan Schwitzer, Richard A. Shaw, J. P. Tyrrell, Jane Vernan and E. J, West.

It is a duty, but above all a pleasure, to thank all those who kindly allowed photography and who submitted with such good grace to the chaos of flashlights, umbrellas, and yards of electric cable. My only regret is that I have not been able to include every interior we photographed. Carol Adams, Tony Adams, Mohamed Al Fayed, Simon Allen, Ian Angus, Pat Astley-Cooper, Sheila Ayres, Michael Bampton, His Excellency Vicomte Luc de la Barre de Nanteuil, G. Bates, Leslie Beaton, Meryl Beaumont, Graham Beck, Robin Bellwood, A. J. Bentley, Michael Bentley and Ronald Jones, Simon Berry, Elizabeth Bowes, Geraldine Bristow, Daria Brown, Michael T Brown, Robert Brown, Caroline Chubb, Stanley Comras, Sir Terence Conran, Chris Cooper, Colin Cooper, Sue Coppins, R. D. Corley, Julian Courtney, Ronald Cowe, Nicholas Crawley, Sue Cross, F. R. Dagnell, Julia Daniels, Paddy Drummond, Mike Dugdale, Michael Eagleton, Mrs Edwards, Mr and Mrs Ferguson, John Field, Peter Fyson, R. A. M. Forrest, Richard Garratt, Gordon Garretty, Myles Glover, John Graham-Leigh, Mr Gwynn, His Excellency Joao Hall Thermido, Peter Hames, Analisa Hamilton, John Harvey, R. Harvey, Paul Herbert, Henry Hoare, Felix Hope-Nicolson, Jean Hudson, Paula Hunt, J. E. Hok, Charles Jencks, Michele Julian, Mrs Killick, Mr Kimpton, Andrew Knight, H. E. Leif Leifland and Mrs Leifland, Mr M. T. N. Liddiard, Fiona

Lindsay, W. Lindsay, David McKinstry, Jane McMorrow, P. Magnavacca, Julian Malone-Lee, Mr Martyn, Christine Mathez, John Mayhew, Christopher Mitchell, John Moran, Jim Morgan, Moira Mullen, Major Munthe, T. W. Nevin, Sister Nora, M. O'Brien, Major Charles O'Leary, John Oliver, D. G. Parry, Richard Parsons, Flight Ltnt Commander Paul Raine, Bill Roberts, Michael A. Roberts, Viscount Rothermere, Jacqueline Seabrook, Denis Seavers, Malcolm Smith, Richard Smith, W. C. Smith, Jeremy de Souza, Derek Stevens, William Stevenson, David Stileman, R. C. G. Strick, Peter Thornton, Annie Traherne, Patrick Trevor-Roper, R. J. Vardy, K. G. Varley, Claire Walsh, Giles Waterfield, Mark Webb, Sandra Weston, David Whisker, Stella Whitborn, Diane Williams, Mr Williams, A. W. Wilson and Mr Wyles.

The book's designer, James Campus, deserves a medal not only for his inspired work on the layout but also for physical endurance, having survived an inner-city ambush in which a good many of the photographs in this book were snatched at knife-point. Thanks are also due to Roger Sears, Editorial Director at Phaidon Press, who first saw the book's potential and who set the wheels in motion; to my editor Deirdre Headon, who kept me in line but never scolded; to my agent Xandra Hardie, whose patience and kindness are boundless; to Mark Fletcher and Sebastian Wormell, who helped compile the gazetteer; to Dolores Karney and Maria Seed, who did such an expert job of typing the manuscript; to all the many friends who accompanied me on long excursions in search of likely locations, especially Katya and Natasha Grenfell (fond memories of 'Maurice' days), Edward Harcourt, Stephen Hermer (who dreamed up the title), Emma-Louise O'Reilly, and David and Nassimah Reynolds; to my mother who took such an interest; and finally to Bridget, who carried me, kicking and screaming, over the final hurdle.

SELECT BIBLIOGRAPHY

HOWARD COLVIN, *A Biographical Dictionary of British Architects 1600–1840,* London, 1978.
MARK GIROUARD, *Victorian Pubs,* London, 1975.
ANTHONY LEJEUNE, *The Gentlemen's Clubs of London,* London, 1979.
IAN NAIRN, *Nairn's London,* London, 1966.
JOHN JULIUS NORWICH, *The Architecture of Southern England,* London, 1985.
SIR NIKOLAS PEVSNER & BRIDGET CHERRY, *Buildings of England Vols I & II,* London, reprinted 1985.
ANNE SAUNDERS, *The Art & Architecture of London,* Oxford, 1984.
ALASTAIR SERVICE, *The Architects of London from 1066 to the Present Day,* London, 1979.
Survey of London.
MALCOM WEBB, *Greater London's Suburban Cinemas,* Birmingham 1986.

GAZETTEER

Although details are correct at the time of going to press, readers are advised to check opening times, etc. before making a visit.

....

SHOPS

R. ALLEN & CO. (BUTCHERS) LTD

Address: 117 Mount Street, W1Y 6HX
Telephone: 01.499 5831
Underground: Marble Arch or Green Park
Open for business: 5 am–4 pm Mon–Fri, 6 am–1 pm Sat.

Built 1886–7 to designs of James Trant-Smith; red brick facade with Queen Anne and Franco-Flemish motifs in terracotta; tiled interior virtually unchanged; famous for traditional shop displays.

AUSTIN REED

Address: 103–113 Regent Street, W1A 2AJ
Telephone: 01.734 6789
Underground: Piccadilly Circus
Open for business: 9 am–5 pm Mon, Wed, Thurs, Fri, 9.30 am–12.45 pm Tues.

Edwardian Baroque exterior designed by Reginald Blomfield; Art Deco Barber Shop in basement completed 1929–30 to designs of P. J. Westwood. Barber's beautifully restored and maintained: vitrolite panelling, Travertine marble floor, original Barber's chairs by Osborne Garrett & Co.

BATES

Address: 21a Jermyn Street, SW1Y 6HP
Telephone: 01.734 2722
Nearest Underground: Piccadilly
Open for business: 9 am–5.30 pm, Mon–Fri, 9.30 am–4 pm Sat. Closed for lunch 1 pm–2 pm.

Typical late Victorian hatter; located on ground floor of Gordon

Chambers, residential/commercial development completed 1897 to designs of Edward Keynes Porchase, architect of Mallett in Bond Street [q.v.].

BERRY BROS.

Address: 3 St James's Street, SW1A 1EG
Telephone: 01.930 1888
Underground: Green Park
Open for business: 9.30 am–5 pm Mon–Fri.

Wine merchants; established late seventeenth century; still in family ownership; site of shop originally occupied by farm house converted 1676 as coffee shop; site redeveloped 1731–5 to create present premises; ground floor interior largely unchanged; wooden floor, panelled walls, weighing beams, shelves lined with old bottles, Victorian furniture; Arts and Crafts Dining Room on first floor with de Morgan tiles.

HARRODS

Address: Brompton Road, SW1X 7XL
Telephone: 01.730 1234
Underground: Knightsbridge
Open for business: 9 am–6 pm Mon–Sat, 9.30 am–7 pm Wed.

One of earliest and best preserved department stores in London; business founded by Henry Charles Harrod 1835; began as grocer's; originally situated in Stepney; moved to Brompton Road Knightsbridge, 1849; gradual expansion to fill present island site 1911; main block erected 1901–03 to designs of Charles W. Stephens, architect of Claridge's [q.v.]; Basil Street façade added by Louis D. Blanc 1929–30; many surviving details within; ornate Edwardian plasterwork in principal interiors along Brompton Road; virtuoso tile work in Meat Hall, executed 1901–03 by Doulton's to designs of W. J. Neatby; Edwardian showcases in Jewellery Department; Classical Revival Luggage Department dating from late 1920s; suite of 1930s interiors in basement below Man's Shop: Jacobean Revival Saloon, Moderne Gentleman's Lavatory, Art Deco Barber Shop; currently under restoration.

MALLETT & SON (ANTIQUES) LTD

Address: 40 New Bond Street, W1 0BS
Telephone: 01.499 7411
Underground: Bond Street
Open for business: 9.15 am–5.15 pm Mon–Fri.

Baroque Revival exterior designed *c.* 1905 by E. Keynes Porchase, architect of Bates [q.v.]; acquired by Mallett; interior with Italianate grotto designed by Raymond Erith 1968.

MALLETT AT BOURDON HOUSE LTD

Address: Bourdon House, Davies Street, W1Y 1LJ
Telephone: 01.629 2444
Underground: Bond Street
Open for business: 9.15am–5.15 pm Mon–Fri.

Early Georgian town house built 1721–25; extended in mid-eighteenth and again in 1909–10;

occupied by Duke of Westminster 1917–53; acquired by Mallett's after Duchess of Westminster's death, 1957; interior well preserved; Georgian Staircase with carved treads and turned balusters; much original woodwork; shellwork grotto by Gordon Davies on first floor, 1975; furnished throughout with finest antiques.

W. MARTYN'S

Address: 135 Muswell Hill, Broadway, N10 3RS
Telephone: 01.883 5642
Underground: Muswell Hill
Open for business: 9 am–5.30 pm Mon–Sat, 9 am–1 pm Thurs.

Established 1897 as general grocer's; now specialising in tea, coffee, and fine foods; known locally as 'Fortnum & Mason of Muswell Hill'; still in family ownership after four generations; interior virtually unchanged; wooden floor and counters, barley twist shelving, late Victorian merchandising.

JAMES SMITH

Address: 53 New Oxford Street, WC1A 1BL
Telephone: 01.836 4731
Underground: Tottenham Court Road
Open for business: 9.30 am–5.20 pm Mon–Fri, 10 am–4 pm occasional Sats.

Umbrella makers; business founded 1830; moved to present premises (former dairy) 1856; shopfront emblazoned with painted signs; interior virtually unchanged since Victorian times.

TESSIERS

Address: 26 New Bond Street,
W1Y 0JY
Telephone: 01.629 6405
Underground: Bond Street
Open for business: 9.30 am–5 pm
Mon–Fri.

Jewellers and silversmiths;
business established in late
eighteenth century by Lewis
Tessier, grandson of Huguenot
exile said to be descended from
Kings of Sicily; present shop
opened by Tessier's sons, 1852;

patronized by Queen Victoria and
other members of royal family; two
changes of ownership before
business acquired by great uncle of
present owners, 1910; shop front
and interior more or less unchanged
since 1852; mahogany and looking-
glass display cases set off by antique
jewellery and silver; Corinthian
columns framing door to rear;
framed locks of hair providing
reminder that Tessiers were
originally 'artists in hair'.

RESTAURANTS

CAFE ROYAL

Address: 68 Regent Street, W1R 6EL
Telephone: 01.734 8520
Underground: Piccadilly Circus
Open for business: 12 noon–3 pm,
6 pm–11 pm daily.

Grill Room completed 1865–72
to designs of Archer & Green,
architects of Hyde Park Hotel;
more or less unchanged despite
reconstruction of building 1923–8
by Sir Henry Tanner, architect of
Park Lane Hotel [q.v.]; jewel box
effect, caryatids, resplendent
mirrors, painted ceiling.

F. COOKE

Address: 41 Kingsland High Street
E8 2JL
Telephone: 01.254 9322
Underground: Dalston Junction
Open for business: 10 am–8 pm
Mon–Sat.

Traditional eel-and-pie shop;
business founded in Hackney 1862
by great-grandfather of present
owner; present restaurant opened
1910; two tons of live eels kept in
tanks on premises; palatial interior,

tiled and mirrored with many
original furnishings; one of the
sights of London.

CRITERION BRASSERIE

Address: 222 Piccadilly, W1 9LB
Underground: Piccadilly Circus
Telephone: 01.839 7133
Open for business: 8.30 am–11 pm
Mon–Sat, 11 am–10.30 pm Sun.

Part of Criterion Theatre
complex, built to designs of
Thomas Verity 1870–74; present
decoration thought to date from *c.*
1905; gilt mosaic ceiling, Moorish
arcades, marble carvings, some
original light fittings; quite
breathtaking.

RISTORANTE ITALIANO

Address: 54–5 Curzon Street,
W1Y 7PF
Telephone: 01.629 2742
Underground: Green Park
Open for business: 11.30 am–3 pm,
5.30–11.30 pm Mon–Fri, 5.30 pm–
11.30 pm Sat.

Rococo Revival interiors of *c.*
1900 located on first floor of
eighteenth-century town house;
fibrous plaster C-scrolls, musical
trophies, etc.; ideal setting for
romantic tête-à-têtes and private
parties.

RULE'S

Address: 35 Maiden Lane, WC2
Telephone: 01.836 5314
Underground: Covent Garden
Open for business: 12 noon–12
midnight Mon–Sat.

Restaurant founded 1798;
interior of present building
completed *c.* 1890; frequented by
King Edward VII and his mistress
Lily Langtry; public and private
dining rooms with immense charm
and period atmosphere; many
original furnishings.

SAGNE MAISON PATISSERIE

Address: 105 Marylebone High
Street, W1M 3DB
Telephone: 01.935 6240
Underground: Baker Street
Open for business: 9 am–5 pm
Mon–Fri, 9 am–12.30 pm Sat.

Founded 1921 by Swiss pastry-
lover M. Sagne; Sagne succeeded by
assistant manager, who sold
business to present owners 1963;
interior retains strong Continental
atmosphere; inlaid woodwork and
murals representing landscapes
with classical ruins.

SIMPSON'S-IN-THE-STRAND

Address: 100 Strand, WC2R 0EW
Telephone: 01.836 9112
Underground: Charing Cross
Open for business: 12 noon–1.30 pm,
6 pm–9 pm Mon–Sat.

Founded 1828; remodelled and
redecorated 1890s by Thomas
Collcutt, architect of Lloyds
Register of Shipping [q.v.]; Adam
Revival interiors on first floor; Arts
and Crafts Dining Room on ground
floor; many original furnishings;
traditional English fare.

HOTELS

CLARIDGE'S

Address: Brook St, W1A 2JQ
Telephone: 01.629 8860
Underground: Bond Street

Hotel founded 1854 by William
and Marianne Claridge, succeeded
by Claridge's Hotel Company 1881;
acquired 1892 by Richard D'Oyly
Carte, theatrical impresario and
owner of Savoy Hotel in Strand;
original building pulled down and
replaced 1895–9; shell designed by
C. W. Stephens, architect of
Brompton Road façade of Harrods
[q.v.]; decoration of interior
entrusted to Sir Ernest George;
1925–6 interior extensively
redecorated by Basil Ionides, who
also worked on Savoy Hotel and
Theatre [q.v.]; 1929–36 alterations
and additions by Oswald Milne;
spectacular public rooms and
private suites beautifully
maintained by management and
staff; surviving decoration and
furniture from 1890s through to
late 1930s.

THE DORCHESTER

Address: Park Lane, W1A 2HJ
Telephone: 01.629 8888
Underground: Hyde Park Corner

Begun to designs of Owen Jones
but completed 1930 by William
Curtis Green, architect of Barclays
Bank, Piccadilly [q.v.]; new wing
added 1953 with penthouse suite by
stage designer Oliver Messel;
Messel rooms little changed; rest of
hotel extensively altered and
modernized; due for drastic
refurbishment.

GREAT EASTERN HOTEL

Address: Liverpool Street,
EC2M 2QN
Telephone: 01.283 4363
Underground: Liverpool Street
Admission to Freemasons' Temple
by prior permission, apply in
writing.

Main block completed to designs
of Charles Barry 1884; Freemasons'
Temple added 1912 by Brown and
Barrow; Temple well preserved
otherwise hotel interior spoilt by
recent refurbishment.

INVERNESS COURT HOTEL

Address: Inverness Terrace, W2 3JL
Telephone: 01.229 1444
Underground: Bayswater or
Queensway

Built around turn of century by
prominent Victorian businessman
for mistress; extraordinary range of
bizarre interiors including
Viennese-style private theatre (now
used as bar), Louis XVI-style Salon,
Victorian Drawing Room, early
Georgian Conference Room, and
Baroque Staircase.

PARK LANE HOTEL

Address: Piccadilly, W1
Telephone: 01.499 6321
Underground: Green Park

Built *c.* 1927 for Yorkshire
magnate Sir Bracewell Smith to
designs by Henry Tanner;
surviving 1920s decoration in Foyer
and Ball Room; some original
furniture.

St. Pancras Hotel

St Pancras Hotel

Address: Euston Road, NW1 2QL
Telephone: 01.247 5444
Underground: King's Cross
Contact British Rail Property
Department on above number
Built 1873–8 to designs by Sir
George Gilbert Scott for London
Midland and Scottish Railway
Company; originally known as
Midland Grand Hotel; closed down
and converted into offices 1935;
hybrid of English and Continental
Gothic; superb ironwork and
stencilled decoration in Staircase
Compartment; many other fine
interiors; awaiting restoration.

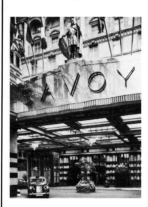

The Savoy

Address: Strand, WC2R 0EU
Telephone: 01.836 4343
Underground: Charing Cross
Stands on site of medieval Palace
of Savoy; built in two stages: first
block along river completed 1889,
second block facing Strand erected
1903–04; exteriors designed by
Thomas Collcutt, architect of
Lloyds Register of Shipping and
Simpson's-in-the-Strand [q.v.];
decoration of interiors entrusted to
Arts and Crafts designer Arthur H.
Mackmurdo; river front suites later
redecorated in Louis XV/Louis
XVI style by Paris *décorateur* René
Sergent; metallic Art Deco fascia
added to Strand front by Murray
Easton and Howard Robertson
1929; public rooms extensively
redecorated 1926–9 by Basil
Ionides, who also worked on
interiors of adjoining Savoy
Theatre and Claridge's [q.v.]; many
surviving details, including
allegorical frieze and foliated
handrails in Foyer (1880s),
dixhuitième panelling and overdoors
in bedrooms overlooking river (*c.*
1905), naval columns and tassel
panelling in Pinafore Room (1920s),
and etched looking-glass recess on
approach to Ball Room (1920s);
some period furniture.

CLUBS & SOCIETIES

*Gentlemen's Clubs are not generally
open to visitors other than members
and their guests but it is worth
applying in writing to the secretary.*

Athenaeum Club

Address: Pall Mall, SW1Y 5ER
Telephone: 01.930 4843
Underground: Piccadilly
Founded as club for artists and
men of letters 1824; designed by
Decimus Burton and completed
1827–30; attic storey added 1899–
1900 by Thomas Collcutt, architect
of Simpson's-in-the-Strand [q.v.];
several splendid interiors, notably
Entrance Hall, Coffee Room
(recently restored), Smoking Room,
and Library; many original
furnishings.

Brooks's

Address: St James's Street,
SW1A 1LN
Telephone: 01.493 4411
Underground: Green Park
Founded 1764; clubhouse built
1776–8 to designs of Henry
Holland; rear annexe by John
MacVicar Anderson 1889;
surviving eighteenth-century
decoration, including painted
panels, plasterwork, chimney
pieces, pier glasses, and
overmantels; Great Subscription
Room (immaculately restored after
fire), Library, and Staircase Hall are
of special interest; fine collection of
portraits and antique furniture.

The Reform Club

Address: Pall Mall, SW1Y 5EW
Telephone: 01.930 9374
Underground: Piccadilly
Club founded 1836 for
champions of electoral reform;
clubhouse erected 1838–41 to

designs of Sir Charles Barry,
architect of House of Lords and
Travellers' Club [q.v.]; exterior
based on Palazzo Farnese in Rome;
interiors of similar extraction:
Great Hall, Library, Morning
Room, and Staircase are very fine;
many original furnishings.

The Royal Automobile Club

Address: 89 Pall Mall, SW1Y 5HS
Telephone: 01.930 2345
Underground: Piccadilly or Green
Park
Club founded 1897 for
'Protection, Encouragement &
Development of Automobilism';
clubhouse designed by Anglo-
French partnership of Arthur Davis
and Charles Mewès, architects of
Ritz Hotel; built 1908–11 on site of
old War Office; Place de la
Concorde exterior and many
splendid interiors, including Louis
XVI-style Dining Room and
Byzantine Swimming-Pool.

The Royal Society

Address: 6 Carlton House Terrace,
SW1Y 5AG
Telephone: 01.839 5561
Underground: Piccadilly
Originally built as palatial town
house by John Nash *c.* 1830; interior
redecorated 1889–90 for Buenos
Aires millionaire C. H. Sanford by
Sir Ernest George; home of Royal
Society since 1967; replica of
Quattrocento Florentine Palazzo;
spectacular marble Entrance Hall
and Staircase, exquisite carvings,
inlaid doors, mother-of-pearl
ceiling, allegorical paintings.

The Travellers' Club

Address: 106 Pall Mall, SW1 5EP
Telephone: 01.930 8688
Underground: Piccadilly
Club founded 1819 'to form a
point of reunion for gentlemen who
have travelled abroad and to afford
them the opportunity of inviting as
honorary visitors the principal
members of all foreign missions and
travellers of distinction'; clubhouse
built 1829–32 by Sir Charles Barry,
architect of Reform Club and
House of Lords [q.v.]; pioneering
exercise in Palazzo style; many
grand interiors, of which library is
most impressive; fine collection of
pictures and furniture.

PUBLIC HOUSES

The Blackfriar

Address: 174 Queen Victoria Street,
EC4V 4BY
Telephone: 01.236 5650

Underground: Blackfriars
Open for business: 11.30am–9 pm,
Mon–Fri.
Uniquely fine example of Arts
and Crafts pub, built 1905 to
designs of architect H. Fuller Clark
and sculptor Henry Poole;
streetfront and interior well
preserved; jolly barrel-vaulted
chamber to rear, decorated with
marble, mosaics, and bronze reliefs
and figures on mock-monastic
theme.

The Bride of Denmark

Address: Architectural Press,
9 Queen Anne's Gate, SW1H 9BY
Telephone: 01.222 4333
Underground: St James's Park
Private bar; *admission* by written
application.
Located in basement of terraced
house built *c.* 1704; suite of
Victorian-style bar rooms
assembled from fragments salvaged
from pubs destroyed in Blitz;
designed *c.* 1949 by committee
headed by Hubert de Cronin
Hastings, editor of Architectural
Review.

The Red Lion

Address: 2 Duke of York Street,
St. James's, SW1 6JY
Telephone: 01.930 2030
Underground: Piccadilly
Open for business: 11 am–11 pm
Mon–Sat, 12 noon–3 pm Sun.
Established in or before 1788;
original pub rebuilt 1821; present
interior designed by W. H.
Rawlings 1871; much original
decoration; lincrusta ceiling,
mahogany woodwork, and
spectacular virtuoso glasswork
attributed to Walter Gibbs & Sons
of Southwark.

The Salisbury

Address: 1 Grand Parade,
Haringay N4
Telephone: 01.800 3600
Underground: Manor House
Open 11 am–11 pm Mon–Sat, 12
noon–3 pm Sun.

Grandiose late Victorian gin palace by north London builder John Cathles Hill; opened 1899; terrazzo floors, stained and etched glass, painted tiles, wrought-ironwork; quite overpowering.

YE OLDE CHESHIRE CHEESE

Address: 145 Fleet Street, EC4E 4BU
Telephone: 01.353 6170
Underground: Blackfriars
Open for business, Bar 11.30 am–11 pm Mon–Fri, Sat same; Restaurant 12 noon–3 pm, 6 pm–9 pm Mon–Fri, Sat same am, 6 pm–8.30 pm, 12 noon–3 pm Sun.

Traditional pub and chop house; erected 1677; street front altered *c*. 1820; reputedly frequented by Dr Johnson, who occupied nearby house in Gough Square [q.v.]; atmospheric interior.

....

DOMESTIC INTERIORS

CHARLTON HOUSE

Address: Charlton House Community Centre, Charlton Road, Charlton SE7 8RE
Telephone: 01.856 3951
Railway Station: Charlton
Admission by written application.

Jacobean manor house built 1607–12 for Sir Adam Newton, tutor to Henry, Prince of Wales, eldest son of James I; attributed to John Thorpe; minor alterations 1659; restored and enlarged by Norman Shaw 1877–8; privately owned until 1925 when acquired by local authority; unusual two-storey Hall; original plasterwork and chimney pieces in Saloon, Long Gallery and White Drawing Room.

NO. 18 FOLGATE STREET

Address: 18 Folgate Street, Spitalfields, E1 6BX
Telephone: 01.247 4013
Underground: Liverpool Street
Admission: Guided tours 3 times weekly. Telephone for details.

Terraced house erected 1724; recently acquired and transformed by American Dennis Severs; ingenious antiquarian interiors in every style of decoration from early eighteenth to late nineteenth century.

HAM HOUSE

Address: Richmond, Surrey TW10 7RS
Telephone: 01.940 1950
Underground: Richmond, then buses 65 or 71 to Fox and Duck Inn, Petersham

Open 11 am–5.pm Tues–Sun inclusive, also Easter Monday, Spring and August Bank Holidays. Closed Mon, 1 January, Good Friday, May Day Bank Holiday, 24, 25, 26 December.

Built 1610 for Sir Thomas Vavasour, Earl Marshal to James I; extensive alterations 1637–9 for William Murray, 1st Earl of Dysart; enlarged and aggrandized 1670s for Dysart's daughter after marriage to Duke of Lauderdale; new furniture added 1727 by 4th Earl of Dysart, who ordered insertion of sash windows; remained in family ownership until 1948 when presented to National Trust; restored to rare degree of accuracy; many fine interiors with original furnishings.

LEIGHTON HOUSE

Address: 12 Holland Park Road, W14 8L7
Telephone: 01.602 3316
Underground: Kensington High Street
Open 11 am–6 pm Mon–Sat.

Begun 1865 as studio and town house for Frederick, Lord Leighton, President of Royal Academy and only English artist to be elevated to peerage; designed by Leighton in partnership with architect George Aitchison; studio extended 1869–70; Arab Hall added 1877–9; converted into museum after Leighton's death; subsequently acquired by local council; several fascinating interiors beautifully restored and cared for by present curator; important collection of Victorian paintings.

LINLEY SAMBOURNE HOUSE

Address: 16 Stafford Terrace, W8 7BH
Telephone: 01.994 1019
Underground: Kensington High St.
Open 10 am–4 pm Wed, 2 pm–5 pm

Sun, Mar–Oct; otherwise by written application to Victorian Society, 1 Priory Gardens, W4.

Victorian terraced house occupied 1874–1910 by Linley Sambourne, chief political cartoonist at *Punch*; remained in family ownership until 1980 when presented to Victorian Society and opened to public; perfectly-preserved example of 'Artistic' style in interior decoration; full complement of original furnishings.

LITTLE HOLLAND HOUSE

Address: 40 Beeches Avenue, Carshalton, Surrey SN5 3LW
Telephone: 01.661 5000
Railway Station: Carshalton Beeches
Open 12 noon–6 pm first Sun of each month Mar–Oct and Sun and Mon of Easter, Spring, and Summer Bank Holiday weekends.

Arts and Crafts house built 1902–04 by original occupant, Frank Dickinson, self-taught artist/craftsman, and visionary disciple of William Morris; acquired from Dickinson's heirs by local authority 1972; virtually unchanged since Dickinson's death; wealth of furniture and artefacts designed and hand-crafted by Dickinson himself.

MARBLE HILL HOUSE

Address: Richmond Road, Twickenham, Middlesex TW1 2NL
Telephone: 01.892 5115
Underground: Richmond
Open 10 am–5 pm daily except Fri (closes 4 pm Nov–Jan).

Palladian villa built 1724–9 for Henrietta Howard, Countess of Suffolk, and mistress of George II; original plan by Colen Campbell; final execution by Roger Morris with assistance from Henry Herbert, later 9th Earl of Pembroke; Dining Room altered 1750–1 by Matthew Brettingham; privately owned until 1902 when acquired by LCC; restored as public museum by GLC 1965–6; restoration continuing; house small but stately, befitting rank of original occupant; incompletely furnished but architectural decoration intact.

THE OCTAGON, ORLEANS HOUSE

Address: Orleans House Gallery, Riverside, Twickenham, Middlesex TW1 3DJ
Telephone: 01.892 0221
Underground: Richmond
Open 1 pm–5.30 pm, Tues–Sat (1 pm–4.30 pm Oct–May); 2 pm–5.30 pm Sun (2 pm–4.30 pm Oct–May); 2 pm–5.30 pm Easter, Spring, Summer Bank Hols. Closed Christmas.
Admission free.

Domed octagonal pavilion built 1720 to designs of James Gibbs with virtuoso plasterwork by Giovanni Bagutti and Giuseppe Artari; setting for official reception of George II's new Queen, Caroline Anspach, 1729; originally situated in grounds of large house built 1710 by John James for James Johnston; house occupied 1815–17 by Louis-Philippe Duc d'Orléans, later King of France, hence name; octagon saved from destruction by Hon. Mrs Levy when house demolished 1927; bequeathed to local authority 1962.

OSTERLEY PARK HOUSE

Address: Isleworth, TW7 4RB
Telephone: 01.560 3918
Underground: Osterley
Open daily 11 am–5 pm except Mon, Good Friday, May Day Bank Holiday, Christmas Eve, Christmas Day, Boxing Day, and New Year's Day.

House of 1578 remodelled for banker Robert Child by Robert Adam 1763–80; privately owned until 1949 when presented to National Trust; restored with great flair and sympathy; many fine interiors with original furnishings.

SIR JOHN SOANE MUSEUM

Address: 13 Lincoln's Inn Fields, WC2 3BP
Telephone: 01.405 2107
Underground: Holborn
Open 10 am–5 pm Tues–Sat inclusive. Closed on Bank Holidays and Christmas Eve.

Early nineteenth-century town house built, occupied and bequeathed to nation by architect Sir John Soane; virtually untouched since Soane's death, 1837; not to be missed.

SOUTHSIDE HOUSE

Address: Woodhayes Road, Wimbledon Common, SW19 4RJ
Telephone: 01.946 7643
Underground: Wimbledon
Guided tours 2 pm–5 pm on the hour Tues, Thurs, Fri, Oct 1–Mar 31; otherwise apply in writing.

Seventeenth-century farm house extensively rebuilt and aggrandized in eighteenth century; still in family ownership; beguiling antiquarian interiors made up of fragments and furnishings from different periods; some perhaps original to house, but most, one imagines, assembled in nineteenth century; fascinating web of fact and fiction.

....

THEATRES AND CINEMAS

For access to auditoria it is best to apply in writing. Foyers are generally open to the street.

THE ACADEMY THEATRE

Address: 211 Stockwell Road, SW9 9SL
Telephone: 01.274 1525
Underground: Brixton
Admission by written application.

Grand 'atmospheric' cinema completed 1929 to designs of Edward A. Stone; seating capacity 2,982; opening show 'The Singing Fool'; closed 1972 with 'Red Sun' and 'The Looking Glass War'; reopened as venue for live shows 1982; half-domed classical entrance hall; Art Deco Foyer; outlandish auditorium with proscenium arch forming Italian Renaissance villa and garden complex, complete with statues, artificial vegetation, and ceiling painted to represent star-lit sky.

THE COLISEUM

Address: St Martin's Lane, WC2N 4ES
Telephone: 01.836 7700
Underground: Trafalgar Square

Lavish music hall built 1903–4 for impresario Oswald Stoll by Frank Matcham, architect of Hackney Empire [q.v.]; occupied since August 1968 by English National Opera; Foyer sadly whitewashed; auditorium well preserved.

HACKNEY EMPIRE

Address: 291 Mare Street, E8 1EJ
Telephone: 01.985 2424
Underground: Bethnal Green
Admission by written application.

Built for theatrical impresario Oswald Stoll by Frank Matcham, architect of Coliseum [q.v.], Sadlers Wells, and Richmond Theatre; opulent interior consciously modelled on grand opera houses of Italy; front of theatre decorated by J. M. Boekbinder; auditorium by De Jong; acquired by Mecca organisation and converted into bingo hall, 1966; taken over by present owners, Hackney Empire Preservation Trust, October 1986; currently under restoration and in need of funds.

NEW RAINBOW THEATRE

Address: Seven Sisters Road, Finsbury Park, N4 3NX
Telephone: 01.281 4182
Underground: Finsbury Park

Originally Astoria, Finsbury Park; 'atmospheric' cinema completed 1930 to designs of Edward A. Stone, architect of Academy Theatre, Brixton [q.v.]; acquired by Odeon chain 1970; closed as cinema 1971; converted into Dance Hall and venue for rock concerts; acquired by New Rainbow Trust 1987; due to be restored.

THE PLAYHOUSE THEATRE

Address: Northumberland Avenue, WC2N 4DE
Telephone: 01.839 4401
Underground: Charing Cross
Admission by written application.

Completed 1906 to designs of Detmar Blow and Fernand Billerey; interior recently restored; drop curtain and painted panels on walls and ceiling of auditorium by Henri Brémond and Maurice Tastemain; allegorical figures over proscenium arch and caryatids supporting boxes by Louis Noël and Déchin.

THEATRE ROYAL DRURY LANE

Address: Catherine Street, WC2B 5JF
Telephone: 01.836 8108
Underground: Aldwych or Covent Garden
Admission by written application.

Built 1811–12 to designs of Benjamin Wyatt; fourth theatre to be erected on site (first erected 1663); interior remodelled 1831 by Samuel Beazley, architect and playwright; auditorium remodelled 1901 by Philip Pilditch and again 1921–2 by J. Emblin-Walker, assisted by Edward Jones and Robert Crombie; Greek Doric vestibule; domed Foyer; Empire style auditorium; large collection of paintings and statues on theatrical theme; parts of building sadly spoilt by recent refurbishment.

SAVOY THEATRE

Address: Strand, WC2
Telephone: 01.836 8888
Underground: Charing Cross
Front entrance *open* to street.
Admission to rear entrance and auditorium by written application.

Built 1884 by C. J. Phipps for Richard D'Oyly Carte, owner of adjoining hotel; interior completely redecorated 1929 by Basil Ionides, who also worked at Savoy Hotel and Claridge's [q.v.], assisted by Gilbert Seale; finest and best preserved theatre of its date in London; due to be restored.

TOOTING GRANADA

Address: 58 Mitcham Road, SW17 9NA
Telephone: 01.672 5717
Underground: Tooting Broadway
Admission by written application.

Originally cinema, now Bingo Club; completed 1931; exterior by Cecil Masey and R. H. Uren; interior by Theodore Komisarjevsky; vast auditorium seating more than 3,000; opening show 'Oh! Oh! Cleopatra!'; closed as cinema 1973 with 'The Good, The Bad, and The Ugly'; medieval-style Foyer; Alhambra Hall of Mirrors; auditorium conceived as Gothic cathedral; many original furnishings, including gold-painted Gothic bench on half-landing of main Staircase.

....

OFFICES

Offices are not generally open to the public but tours can sometimes be arranged and it is worth applying in writing for details.

LICHFIELD HOUSE (CLERICAL MEDICAL AND GENERAL LIFE ASSURANCE SOCIETY)

Address: 15 St James's Square, SW1Y 4LQ
Telephone: 01.930 5474
Underground: Green Park
Admission by written application.

Neo-classical town house built 1764–6 for Thomas Anson by James 'Athenian' Stuart; first terraced house in London with Greek temple façade; alterations 1791–4 for Anson's son by Samuel Wyatt; acquired 1856 by Clerical Medical and General Life Assurance Society and converted for use as office block; ground floor extensively remodelled 1928; several interiors with surviving decoration by Stuart and Wyatt, most complete being Board Room and Committee Room.

CROMWELL HOUSE

Address: The Bank, 104 Highgate Hill, N6
Underground: Archway
Open: Apply in writing to architects, Garden & Godfrey, 81 Blackfriars Road, SE1.

Family house built *c.* 1640; extensively restored after fire, 1866; virtuoso brick exterior; Staircase Compartment with surviving seventeenth-century woodwork; currently under restoration.

DAILY EXPRESS

Address: Fleet Street, EC4P 4JT
Telephone: 01.353 8000
Underground: Blackfriars

Futuristic office block built 1931–2 by Ellis, Clarke and Atkinson in partnership with Sir Owen Williams; outlandish Art Deco Entrance Hall designed by Robert Atkinson with metal-work reliefs representing colonial enterprise, chromium handrails forming twisted serpents, and ribbed ceiling with pendentive bosses recalling interior of medieval chapter house.

DAILY MAIL

Address: Carmelite House, Carmelite Street, EC4Y 0JA
Telephone: 01.353 6000
Underground: Blackfriars

Completed 1899 to designs of Herbert Ellis and William Clarke; Art Nouveau murals and elaborate ironwork lift shaft and balustrade in Staircase Hall; Napoleonic Board Room with pedimented mahogany bookcases surmounted by classical murals, *c.*1905.

KENT HOUSE
(EAGLE STAR)

Address: 22 Arlington Street, SW1A 1RW
Telephone: 01.493 8411
Underground: Green Park
Admission by written application.

Palladian town house completed 1755 to designs of William Kent for then Prime Minister, Henry Pelham; building remodelled 1840–52 by Owen Jones and refaced 1854–6 by William Burn for 11th Duke of Hamilton; purchased 1870 by millionaire industrialist Ivor Bertie Guest, later Lord Wimborne, and extensively altered and enlarged; turned over 1939 to Red Cross; acquired 1946 by Eagle Star Insurance Co; in recent years restored; sumptuous range of period interiors dating from mid-eighteenth to early twentieth century.

LLOYDS
REGISTER OF SHIPPING

Address: 71 Fenchurch Street, EC3M 4BS
Telephone: 01.709 9166
Undergound: Monument
Admission to entrance hall during office hours 9 am–5.30 pm; visitors should make themselves known to doorman.

Built 1900–01 to designs of Thomas Collcutt, architect of

Simpson's-in-the-Strand [q.v.]; extraordinary cross between Edwardian Baroque and Arts and Crafts; principal interior with murals and ceiling paintings by Frank Brangwyn, Gerald Moira, and E. J. Lambert; surviving decoration also in Library and Staircase Hall.

SPENCER HOUSE
(J. ROTHSCHILD HOLDINGS)

Address: 27 St James's Place, SW1A 1NW
Telephone: 01.493 8111
Underground: Green Park
Admission by written application.

Early Neoclassical town house built 1755–65 for John, 1st Earl Spencer; shell erected and ground floor decorated 1755–8 by John Vardy, pupil of William Kent, under supervision of General George Gray, amateur architect and Secretary of Society of Dilettanti; first floor decorated and in part remodelled 1758–66 by James 'Athenian' Stuart, architect of Lichfield House [q.v.]; ground floor redecorated and in part remodelled for 2nd Earl Spencer 1785–92 by Henry Holland, architect of Brooks's Club [q.v.]; first floor restored and ground floor redecorated by Philip Hardwick 1850s; ground floor redecorated by Parisian *tapissier* 1871; handed over to National Nursing Agency in Second World War; doors, chimney pieces, chair rails, and other fixtures removed to Althorp for safe keeping during Blitz and subsequently incorporated into state apartments there; house let since War to Christie's, British Oxygen Company, Economist Magazine, and most recently, J. Rothschild Holdings; original plasterwork and some woodwork in principal apartments on ground and first floors; painted panels and murals in Painted Room; currently under restoration.

OAK ROOM
(THAMES WATER AUTHORITY)

Address: New River Head, Rosebery Avenue, EC1R 4TP
Telephone: 01.837 3300
Underground: Angel
Admission by written application.

Late seventeenth-century panelled interior located in 1920s office block; superb carving by Grinling Gibbons, exuberant Baroque plasterwork, and allegorical portrait of William III on ceiling by court painter Henry Cooke; originally part of Cistern House (name later changed to Water House), built 1613 on same site as headquarters of New River Company, privately owned business which with technical assistance of engineer Hugh Myddelton and financial backing of James I brought fresh water to London via twenty-mile channel from Hertfordshire to supplement diminishing local supplies; New River Company taken over 1902 by Metropolitan Water Board which purchased Oak Room 1904 for £2,000; Water House torn down 1920 and replaced by present building designed by Austen Hall; Oak Room saved from destruction and incorporated into new structure; slightly altered in process; dismantled and stored during Blitz; reinstated 1945; Metropolitan Water Board absorbed by Thames Water 1973.

NO. 8 CLIFFORD STREET
(WARD LOCK)

Address: 8 Clifford Street, W1X 1RB
Telephone: 01.734 9511
Underground: Green Park
Admission by written application.

Grand town house built 1719; occupied until 1748 by Thomas Walker MP, art-lover and high-ranking government official; remained in family ownership until 1830 when sold to Bethel Walrond who later married daughter of Earl of Rosslyn; in use as tailor's showroom and workshop 1850; divided up into rented units by 1900; acquired 1931 by J. Lyons & Co., and converted into tea shop; currently in use as office building; remarkable for original painted staircase compartment attributed to Sir James Thornhill; later decorative painting on first floor.

....

BANKS

BANK OF ENGLAND

Address: Threadneedle Street, EC2 R8AH

Telephone: 01.601 4878
Underground: Bank
Apply in writing to Public Liaison Group.

Bank founded 1694; operated at first from Mercers' Hall, then from Grocers' Hall; present site acquired 1724; first building completed 1732 to designs of George Sampson; enlarged by Sir Robert Taylor 1764–6 and by Sir John Soane 1788–1808; extensively remodelled and enlarged by Sir Herbert Baker 1921–37; nationalized 1946; little surviving decoration besides Taylor Court Room, hoisted by Baker from ground to first floor and 'improved'.

BARCLAYS
PICCADILLY BRANCH

Address: 160 Piccadilly, W1A 2AB
Telephone: 01.930 2383
Underground: Green Park
Banking hall *open* 9.30–3.30 pm Mon–Fri.

Built 1922 to designs of William Curtis Green, architect of Dorchester Hotel [q.v.]; originally car showroom for Wolseley Motors Ltd; acquired by Barclays 1926 and converted for use as bank by original architect; exotic oriental-style interiors with matching furniture.

C. HOARE & CO

Address: 37 Fleet Street, EC4 P4DQ
Telephone: 01.353 4522
Underground: Aldwych or Temple
Banking hall *open* 9.30–3.30pm
Mon–Fri.

Family-owned bank founded in or before 1673; premises on present site since 1690; present building begun 1829 to designs of Charles Parker; alterations and additions 1929 by Herbert Baker; main block largely unchanged since early nineteenth century; restrained Italianate façade; Classical Banking Hall with stone floor, oak panelling, original oil-burning stove with Greek Revival frieze of gilded honeysuckle and porters in period costume; museum room in preparation on first floor.

LLOYDS
LAW COURTS BRANCH

Address: 222 The Strand,
WC2R IBB
Telephone: 01.583 8641
Underground: Aldwych or Temple
Banking hall *open;* 9.30–3.30pm
Mon–Fri.

Originally a restaurant and club for lawyers; designed by W. Wimble and Goymour Cuthbert; completed 1883; acquired by Lloyds 1895; entrance decorated with Doulton tiles representing flowers and characters from history and literature; remains of similar decoration within.

....

HOSPITALS

GROVELANDS PRIORY HOSPITAL

Address: The Bourne, Southgate,
N14 6RA
Telephone: 01.882 8191
Underground: Southgate

Neo-classical villa built for Walker Gray by John Nash 1798; privately owned until 1902 when acquired by local authority; converted for use as war hospital in 1916 and later incorporated into Royal Northern Hospital; occupied since 1985 by private clinic; fine grisaille panels representing classical scenes in Entrance Hall; handsome Staircase Hall;

remarkable vaulted Breakfast Room painted to represent interior of aviary set in idyllic landscape.

ROYAL HOSPITAL

Address: Royal Hospital Road,
SW3 4SL
Telephone: 01.730 0161
Underground: Sloane Square
Open: 10 am–12 noon, 2 pm–4 pm daily, except Bank Holiday weekends and Sun, Oct–Mar.

Hostel for invalided and veteran soldiers; founded by Charles II 1682; Grand Hall and Chapel designed by Sir Christopher Wren 1682–92; alterations to officer's apartments by Robert Adam 1765–92; minor buildings added by Sir John Soane; Hall and Chapel with fine woodwork and painted decoration; plain but handsome wards (usually not open to the public).

ST. THOMAS'S OLD OPERATING THEATRE

Address: 9a St. Thomas's Street,
SE1 9RY
Telephone: 01.739 2372
Underground: London Bridge
Admission: 12.30–4 pm Mon, Wed, Fri.

Located in attic of chapter house of Southwark Cathedral; originally part of Guy's Hospital and used at one time as herb garret by house apothecary; converted for use as operating theatre 1821; unique example of its kind; gruesome but authentic.

....

SCHOOLS AND COLLEGES

COURTAULD INSTITUTE

Address: Home House, 20 Portman Square, W1H 0BE
Telephone: 01.935 9292
Underground: Bond Street
Admission by prior appointment.

Neo-classical town house built 1773–6 for Dowager Countess of Home by Robert Adam; occupied since 1931 by Courtauld Institute, art history faculty founded by millionaire collector Samuel Courtauld; extremely well preserved despite conversion; inlaid doors, marble chimney pieces, delicate plasterwork, painted panels by Angelica Kauffmann and Zucchi.

HARROW SCHOOL

Address: 1 High Street, Harrow-on-the-Hill, Harrow HA1 3HW
Telephone: 01.422 2196
Underground: Harrow-on-the-Hill
Admission by prior appointment.

School founded 1572 by John Lyon, local yeoman farmer; original building erected 1608–15 to provide assembly hall and class room (Fourth Form Room) for forty boys who originally made up school; Fourth Form Room more or less untouched, except for panelling, on which boys have been allowed to carve their names; graffiti by Byron, Sheridan, Trollope, Peel, and Churchill; also of interest Speech Room and Vaughan Library.

RICHMOND FELLOWSHIP

Address: 8 Addison Road, W14 8DL
Telephone: 01.603 6373
Underground: Holland Park
Admission by written application.

Peacock-coloured town house built for millionaire department store owner Sir Ernest Debenham, by Arts and Crafts architect, Halsey Ricardo; plasterwork by Ernest Gimson; stained glass by Edward Prior; woodwork by William Aumonier; glazed tiles by William de Morgan; interior, Principal Hall, with mosaic ceiling added 1913 by Gaetano Meo and Byzantine-style stone carvings by George Jack; many other good rooms, notably Library, Drawing Room, and Shower Room.

ST MARY'S COLLEGE

Address: Strawberry Hill, Waldegrave Road, Twickenham, TW1 5SX
Telephone: 01.892 0051
Railway Station: Strawberry Hill
Admission: by prior appointment.

Pioneering Gothic Revival villa originally occupied by wit and dilettante, Horace Walpole; begun *c.* 1747; designed by 'Committee of Taste' presided over by Walpole himself and numbering among its members Richard Bentley and John Chute; Robert Adam at work in 1760s; office wing added 1779 by James Wyatt; Victorian wing added by chatelaine and amateur architect, Frances, Lady Waldegrave, 1860–2; most impressive interiors are Gallery, Holbein Bedroom, Library, and Little Chapel.

ST PHILOMENA'S CONVENT

Address: Carshalton House, Pound Street, Carshalton SN5 3PS
Telephone: 01.642 0287

Railway Station: Carshalton
Admission: contact Sutton Library on 01.661 5050 for details.

Built 1713 for Edward Carleton; acquired soon after by Dr. John Radcliffe, physician to Quen Anne; converted for use as school, 1848; occupied since 1893 by St. Philomena's Convent School; bathroom and water tower dating from 1719–20; original Painted Parlour with walls, doors, and shutters depicting landscapes; fine woodwork in Blue Drawing Room, c. 1750.

WESTMINSTER SCHOOL

Address: Ashburnham House, 6 Little Dean's Yard, SW1P 3PB
Telephone: 01.222 4217
Underground: St. James's Park
Open: during Easter holidays. Telephone for details.

Fifteenth-century Prior's lodging remodelled *c.* 1662 for William Ashburnham; acquired by Westminster School 1883; elegant Classical staircase attributed to John Webb (1611–72), pupil of Inigo Jones; also Cotton Library.

....

GOVERNMENT & CIVIC BUILDINGS

DEPTFORD TOWN HALL

Address: New Cross Road, SE14 6AE
Telephone: 01.692 1288
Underground: New Cross
Admission by written application.

Built 1902–05 to designs of Charles E. Rickards; florid Baroque decoration on maritime theme highlighting Deptford's connections with Port of London; principal interiors Staircase Hall.

FOREIGN & COMMONWEALTH OFFICE

Address: King Charles Street, SW1A 2AH
Telephone: 01.270 3000
Underground: Westminster
Admission by written application.

Completed 1866; overall plan by George Gilbert Scott; many fine interiors, notably principal Staircase Hall (currently under restoration), Foreign Secretary's office, Council Chamber of India Office, and Durbar Court; Durbar Court designed by Matthew Digby Wyatt with majolica friezes by Minton, Hollins & Co., recently restored and available for hire.

HOUSE OF LORDS

Address: Parliament Square, SW1A 0PW
Telephone: 01.219 3000

Underground: Westminster
Admission: British nationals should apply in writing to their local M.P., foreign visitors should contact their embassy or consulate.

Built to designs of Sir Charles Barry, assisted by Augustus Pugin, 1840–70; occupies site of ancient Palace of Westminster, built for Edward the Confessor in mid-eleventh century and destroyed by fire 1834; tour de force of Gothic Revival architecture; majestic interior exhibiting work of greatest artist-craftsmen of day.

LANCASTER HOUSE

Address: Stable Yard, St James's, SW1A 1BB
Telephone: 01.798 4023
Underground: Green Park
Admission 2 pm–6 pm Sat and Sun late Spring–early Autumn. The house may be closed at short notice for Government functions; ring in advance.

Begun 1825 for Frederick, Duke of York, second son of George III, to designs of Benjamin Wyatt; unfinished at time of York's death and purchased by Government; leased to Marquis of Stafford, later Duke of Sutherland; 1833–8 house completed under supervision of Sir Robert Smirke, architect of British Museum, who added attic storey; Staircase Hall remodelled *c.* 1838 by Sir Charles Barry, architect of Travellers' Club, Reform Club and House of Lords [q.v.]; house sold 1912 by Sutherland's heirs to Sir William Lever, who presented it to nation as centre for government hospitality; lavish Louis Revival and Italian Palazzo style interiors in excellent state of preservation.

WESTMINSTER HALL

Address: Parliament Square, SW1A 0PW
Telephone: 01.219 3000
Underground: Westminster
Admission: British nationals should apply in writing to their local M.P., foreign visitors should contact their embassy or consulate.

Built for Richard II by mason Henry Yevele and carpenter Hugh Herland, 1395–1403; stands on site of earlier hall built for William Rufus, 1097–99; scene of momentous events in English history, including trials of Sir Thomas More, Guy Fawkes, and Charles I; restored by Sir Charles Barry after fire of 1834; survived both Blitz and recent fire-bomb; interior little changed in almost 600 years; vast hammerbeam roof ornamented with angels bearing shields; stone carvings representing Kings of England.

LIVERY HALLS

WORSHIPFUL SOCIETY OF APOTHECARIES

Address: The Hall, Blackfriars Lane, EC4V 6EJ
Telephone: 01.236 1180
Underground: Blackfriars

Hall available for hire; occasional open days; apply in writing for details. Society granted charter by James I 1617; main block completed 1669–71 to designs of Thomas Locke with woodwork by Robert Byrges and Roger Davis; street front erected 1684 but altered 1779; original brickwork extensively stuccoed 1786; minor alterations in nineteenth century; imposing hall with original reredos and panelling; unusual and finely wrought balustrade on main staircase; seventeenth- and eighteenth-century decoration in Court Room, Library, and Parlour; fine collection of antique medicinal jars.

WORSHIPFUL COMPANY OF ARMOURERS AND BRAZIERS

Address: Armourers Hall, 81 Coleman Street, EC2 5BJ
Telephone: 01.606 1199
Underground: Bank

Company instituted 1322; granted livery company charter 1453; original pre-Fire of London Hall pulled down 1840 and replaced by modest Neo-classical building designed by T. H. Good.

WORSHIPFUL COMPANY OF DRAPERS

Address: Drapers' Hall, EC2N 2DQ
Telephone: 01.588 5001
Underground: Bank

Hall available for hire; occasional open days; apply in writing for details.

Company established 1180; moved to present site 1541; original hall destroyed in Great Fire; much

Worshipful Company of Fishmongers

subsequent rebuilding and redecoration; present structure dates in main from 1868–9 and was designed by Herbert Williams with decorative sculpture by E. W. Wyon; entrance front by Sir T. G. Jackson 1898–9; marble and alabaster Staircase Hall by same; magnificent Livery Hall with ceiling painted 1903–10 with allegories and scenes from Shakespeare; Court Drawing Room, 1869, with original furniture.

WORSHIPFUL COMPANY OF FISHMONGERS

Address: The Hall, London Bridge, EC4R 9EL
Telephone: 01.626 3531
Underground: Monument
Three open days a year; apply in writing for details.

Company established thirteenth century; on or near present site since 1434; original hall destroyed in Great Fire; second hall pulled down 1827 to make way for London Bridge; present hall completed 1834 to designs of Henry Roberts assisted by George Gilbert Scott; restored 1929 by Goodhart-Rendel; damaged in Blitz and again restored by Austen Hall 1951; splendid Greek Revival interiors, particularly Entrance Hall, Staircase Hall, Banqueting Hall, Drawing Room, and Court Room; many original furnishings.

WORSHIPFUL COMPANY OF STATIONERS AND NEWSPAPER MAKERS

Address: Stationers' Hall, Ave Maria Lane, EC4M 7DD
Telephone: 01.248 2934
Underground: St Paul's
Hall available for hire, otherwise closed to visitors.

Stationers' guild formed 1403; granted livery company charter 1557; original hall destroyed in Great Fire; present building completed 1673, to designs of Stephen Colledge; street front refaced 1800 by Robert Mylne; new wing added 1887; damaged in Blitz and subsequently restored; original seventeenth-century panelling and carved oak screen in Hall, accompanied by late nineteenth-century stained glass windows on literary theme; seventeenth-century panelling and chimney piece in Stock Room; original chimney piece in Court Room.

The following list is of interiors which could not be included among the photographs in this book but which are of interest and open to the public.

BANQUETING HOUSE

Address: Whitehall, SW1A 2ER
Underground: Embankment
Open 10 am–5 pm Tues–Sat, Spring and Summer Bank Holiday, 2 pm–5 pm Sun.

Majestic double cube interior by Inigo Jones with ceiling paintings by Rubens.

CARLYLE'S HOUSE

Address: 24 Cheyne Row, SW3 5HL
Telephone: 01.352 7087
Underground: Sloane Square
Open 11 am–5 pm Wed–Sat and Bank Holiday Mon, Apr–Oct, 2 pm–5 pm Sun, Apr–Oct.

Terraced house of 1708 occupied by English historian Thomas Carlyle, 1834–81; well-preserved interior with many original features.

CHARTERHOUSE

Address: Charterhouse Square EC1M 6AN
Telephone: 01.253 9503
Underground: Barbican
Open 3 pm–5 pm Wed, Apr–Jul.

Fourteenth-century Carthusian monastery converted into private house in reign of Henry VIII and into almshouse and school in early seventeenth century; meticulously restored after bomb damage in Blitz; surviving Carthusian cloister and cell; sixteenth-century Great Hall.

CHISWICK HOUSE

Address: Burlington Lane, Chiswick W4 2RP
Telephone: 01.994 3299
Underground: Turnham Green
Open 9.30 am–6.30 pm Mar–Oct, daily 9.30–4.00 pm Oct–Mar.

Model Palladian villa with surviving architectural decoration by William Kent and 3rd Earl of Burlington, *c.* 1726–9.

COLLEGE OF ARMS

Address: Queen Victoria Street EC4V 4BT
Telephone: 01.248 2762
Underground: Blackfriars or Mansion House
Open 10 am–4 pm Mon–Fri throughout year, except public holidays, state, and special occasions.

Headquarters of England's heralds; building erected 1671–88; particularly impressive are Earl Marshal's Court (early eighteenth century) and adjoining Library (late seventeenth century).

CROSSNESS BEAM ENGINE HOUSE

Address: Belvedere Road, Thamesmead, DA2 9AQ
Telephone: 01.310 1116
Railway Station: Abbey Wood, then Bus 272
Admission by prior appointment, telephone for details.
  Outstanding Victorian ironwork and engineering structures.

CROYDON PALACE

Address: Old Palace Road, Croydon, Surrey CR0 1AX
Telephone: 01.680 5877
Railway station: West Croydon
Admission: apply in writing to The Secretary, Friends of Croydon Palace, at above address.
  Former archbishop's palace with twelfth-century undercroft and surviving Hall built in reign of Henry VI.

DICKENS' HOUSE MUSEUM AND LIBRARY

Address: 48 Doughty Street, WC1N 2LF
Telephone: 01.405 2127
Underground: Russell Square
Open 10 am–5 pm Mon–Sat.
  Georgian terraced house occupied by novelist Charles Dickens 1837–9; some original furnishings, memorabilia.

DULWICH PICTURE GALLERY

Address: College Road, SE21 7AD
Telephone: 01.693 5254
Railway Station: West Dulwich
Open 10 am–1 pm, 2 pm–5 pm Tues–Sat, 2 pm–5 pm Sun.
  Oldest public art gallery in England; austere interiors by Sir John Soane, including mausoleum, 1811–4.

ELTHAM PALACE

Address: Eltham, SE9 5NR
Telephone: 01.854 2242
Open 10 am–12 noon, 2.15 pm–6 pm Thurs and Sun (Oct–4 Mar).
  Former royal palace; Tudor Hall with hammerbeam roof, *c.* 1480.

FENTON HOUSE

Address: Windmill Hill, NW3 6RT
Telephone: 01.435 3471
Underground: Hampstead
Open: 11 am–5 pm Sat-Wed, 1 Apr–31 Oct, 2 pm–5 pm Sat and Sun, Mar.
  Late seventeenth-century house with modest panelled interiors containing important collection of early keyboard instruments.

FORTY HALL MUSEUM

Address: Forty Hill, Enfield, EN2 9HA
Telephone: 01.363 8169
Railway Station: Enfield Town, then Buses 231 or 191
Open 10 am–5 pm Tues–Sun, 1 Oct–Easter, 10 am–6 pm Tues–Sun, Easter–31 Sept.
  Jacobean manor house built 1629–36, original carved screen in Hall; elaborate chimney pieces and plasterwork.

GEFFRYE MUSEUM

Address: Kingsland Road, E2 8EA
Telephone: 01.739 8368
Underground: Liverpool Street or Old Street
Open 10 am–5 pm Tues–Sat, 2 pm–5 pm Sun, Bank Holiday Mon.
  Early eighteenth-century alms houses converted into museum of furniture and architectural decoration; reconstructions of English domestic interiors from Elizabethan times to 1930s.

HAMPTON COURT PALACE

Address: East Molesey, Surrey, KT8 9AU
Telephone: 01.997 9447
Railway Station: Hampton Court
Open 9.30 am–6 pm daily, 28 Mar–22 Oct, 9.30 am–4.30 am daily, 23 Oct–27 Mar.
  Begun in early sixteenth century by Cardinal Wolsey; enlarged by Henry VIII after Wolsey's disgrace; largely completed by Sir Christopher Wren for William and Mary; early eighteenth-century addition by Sir John Vanbrugh and William Kent; state apartments opened to public by Queen Victoria 1838; surviving features from every phase of construction.

DR JOHNSON'S HOUSE

Address: 17 Gough Square, EC4 3DE
Telephone: 01.353 3745
Underground: Chancery Lane
Open 11 am–5.30 pm Mon–Sat, 1 May–30 Sept, 11 am–5 pm Mon–Sat, 1 Oct–30 April.
  Early Georgian town house occupied by man of letters, Samuel Johnson, 1748–59; interiors restored in period.

KENSINGTON PALACE STATE APARTMENTS

Address: Kensington Gardens, W8 4PX
Telephone: 01.937 9561 ext. 20
Underground: Kensington High Street
Open 9 am–5 pm Mon–Sat, 1–5 pm Sun, Bank Holidays.
  Magnificent interiors ranging from reign of William and Mary to that of Queen Victoria.

KENWOOD HOUSE, IVEAGH BEQUEST

Address: Hampstead Lane, NW3 7JR
Telephone: 01.348 1286
Underground: Golders Green or Highgate, then bus
Open 10 am–5 pm daily, 1 Apr–30 Sept, 10 am–4 pm daily, 1 Oct–31 Mar.
  Fine Neoclassical interiors by Robert Adam dating from 1760s; important collection of pictures and furniture.

KEW PALACE

Address: Kew, Richmond, Surrey, TW9 3AB
Telephone: 01.940 3321
Underground: Kew
Open 11 am–5.30 pm daily, 1 Apr–30 Sept.
  Seventeenth-century gabled house remodelled in eighteenth century as suburban retreat for George III and Queen Charlotte; modest but distinguished interiors.

MIDDLE TEMPLE HALL

Address: Middle Temple Lane, EC4Y 9AT
Telephone: 01.353 4355
Underground: Temple
Open 10 am–11.30 am, 3 pm–4 pm Mon–Fri, except August.
  Hall built 1562–70; original carved screen and double hammerbeam roof.

NATURAL HISTORY MUSEUM

Address: Cromwell Road, South Kensington, SW7 5BD
Telephone: 01.589 6323
Underground: South Kensington
Open 10 am–6 pm Mon–Sat, 1 pm–6 pm Sun.
  Breath-taking late nineteenth-century interiors by Alfred Waterhouse.

NATIONAL MARITIME MUSEUM

Address: Romney Road, Greenwich, SE10 9NF
Telephone: 01.858 4422
Railway Station: Greenwich
Open 10 am–6 pm Mon–Sat, 12 noon–6 pm Sun, 1 Apr–30 Sept; 10 am–5 pm Mon–Sat, 12 noon–5 pm Sun, 1 Oct–31 Mar.
  Incorporating Queen's House with Palladian interiors by John Webb, pupil of Inigo Jones, 1664–9 (closed for restoration); Royal Naval College with early eighteenth-century Dining Hall by Wren (assisted by Nicholas Hawksmoor) decorated with allegorical wall and ceiling paintings by Sir James Thornhill, early Greek Revival Chapel by James 'Athenian' Stuart 1780–8.

PITSHANGER MANOR MUSEUM

Address: Mattock Lane, Ealing, W5 5EQ
Telephone: 01.579 2424
Underground: Ealing Broadway
Admission: Telephone for details.
  Neoclassical villa with surviving decoration by George Dance (Drawing Room and Eating Room of 1768) and Sir John Soane (Breakfast Room of *c.* 1803).

RED HOUSE

Address: 13 Red House Lane, Bexleyheath, Kent DA6 8JF
Railway station: Bexleyheath
Open one weekday each month, apply in writing.
  Arts and Crafts interiors by William Morris and Philip Webb, *c.* 1860.

SWAKELEY'S HOUSE

Address: The Avenue, Ickenham, Middlesex
Telephone: 0895.639911
Underground: Ickenham
Open three days a year, telephone for details.
  Jacobean manor house built in 1629–38; original carved screen in Hall; Staircase compartment frescoed with scenes from antiquity.

SYON HOUSE

Address: Syon Park, London Road, Brentford, TW8 8JF
Telephone: 01.560 0884
Underground: Gunnersbury, then buses 237 or 267
Open 12 noon–5 pm Sun–Thur, Apr–Aug.
  Fifteenth-century convent remodelled in mid-eighteenth century by Robert Adam; sumptuous Neo-classical interiors.

VICTORIA AND ALBERT MUSEUM

Address: Cromwell Road, SW7 2RL
Telephone: 01.589 6371
Underground: South Kensington
Open 10 am–5.30 pm Mon–Thurs and Sat, 2.30 pm–5.50 pm Sun.
  Many fine interiors, including William Morris Rooms.

WELLINGTON MUSEUM

Address: Apsley House, 149 Piccadilly, W1V 9FA
Telephone: 01.499 5676
Underground: Hyde Park Corner
Open 11 am–5 pm Tues–Sun, Bank Holidays (except May Day).
  London home of 1st Duke of Wellington 1817–52; Neoclassical interiors by Robert Adam; 'Louis XIV' interiors by Benjamin Wyatt; superb collection of porcelain.

INDEX